LEADERS BUILD BUSINESS

Effectively Mentor & Coach Your Sales Team

ADELLA PASOS

Published by Adella Pasos

Copyright © 2020 www.adellapasos.com

All rights reserved. No part of this book, including interior design, cover design, and icons may be reproduced or transmitted in any form, by any means (electronic, photocopying, recording or otherwise) without the prior written permission of the author, except for the inclusion of brief quotations in a review.

CONTENTS

Introduction 1

Chapter 1: Why A Sales Team is Important 3

Chapter 2: The Sales Team Structure 23

Chapter 3: How to Support a Sales Team 53

Chapter 4: Developing Sales Leaders to Improve Results 71

Chapter 5: Ways to Keep the Sales Team Happy 92

Chapter 6: How to Effectively Reduce Sales Team Turnover 108

Chapter 7: How to Choose: 127

Chapter 8: Sales and Marketing Alignment 134

Chapter 9: Measuring Results and Sales Impact 137

Chapter 10: Getting the Best Outcome 142

CONCLUSION 145

Introduction

Throughout the course of this book you will learn how to create, grow and cultivate a group of people with the right combination of skills to take your business to the next level. Throughout my career, I worked with several members of executive teams and business stakeholders. Each encounter allowed me the opportunity to help them learn the art of fostering a good sense of teamwork.

Everything that I experienced, I put into this book to help you lay the foundations for an incredibly successful team, capable of partnering, collaborating, and innovating in an atmosphere of trust and understanding.

The term "leader" means different things, to different people. Some people define it as a quality that only belongs to people with significant political or financial power. Others assume that "leading" can only be done by the achievement of a particular title such as CEO, president, or mayor. What you should always remember is, everyone has the potential to develop qualities of leadership.

Great leaders have the capacity to motivate others to accomplish and crush their goals. A leader is a person who affects others' thoughts and behaviors by using imagination, inspiration, commitment, and collaborative team building to accomplish objectives.

Becoming a leader does not necessarily mean having "all" the power. Because not all people in a position of power have the ability to drive change. The first step in becoming a leader is establishing what you want to achieve. Once you do this, you'll understand the direction in which you'll need to go.

CHAPTER 1

Why A Sales Team is Important

What makes a good sales team?

Many companies today are working hard to develop productive sales teams that outperform their competitors. Creating a working atmosphere in which people stay motivated and want to *actually* participate is not always a walk in the park. However, the question still remains, how do you actually build a great team?

In a team-oriented environment, individual contributions are required to help the team and the organization progress. Each team member will become more and more satisfied when they are able to work in a completely sales focused, supportive environment.

But, how do you give them what they need to be successful? It's not easy to develop teams. Plenty of effort and time should be invested to achieve the performance that a sales team will need to produce. Here are a few simple tips to get you on the fast track to creating a great sales team.

Communication

Communication is the most critical part of creating a sales team. This helps people concentrate on their commitments for the day, week, month, or even longer. It is essential to have a system in place where people get, give, and receive honest feedback from each other. The development of an 'employee' community in which team members are able to connect effectively and socially will also help to create a stronger sales team.

Consequences and Rewards

Employee compensation and commissions have an effect on the activities and performance of team leaders. When a team member achieves something fantastic, a reward for the accomplishment should be recognized as something to aspire for.

Conversely, if there is a moment when a participant lets the team down, adequate punishment should be given. Do not consider a harsh punishment, but just the kind of penalty that the team and the person will learn from their mistakes and improve further.

The Committed Team

Group leaders must dedicate themselves to making the team successful. This sign of dedication and support indicates the leader's willingness to make sure the team will remain focused, keep commitments and meet the sales goals. A good leader's work will always be remembered. Regular preparation, resources, and coaching is essential to sustaining a motivated and dedicated sales team.

Innovation

A creative team that is continually searching for ways to develop helps to build an outstanding team. Assessing the contributions of team leaders who may have an exciting concept helps create this community and rejoices imaginative team members. Innovative sales teams always come up with new and creative solutions to any issue and may eventually overdo teams who concentrate on one thing and do not want to change their ways.

Feeling Competent

When the team doesn't really feel confident, or up to the roles it was assigned, it will crumble easily into a negative attitude. When the team sees a deficiency in a particular purpose or mission, the easiest fix is to provide a solution like tailored training. Access to the correct tools often leads to improved competences, and the lack of them can build a serious issue.

How Does a Sales Team Work?

History is often said to have repeat itself, so there is no "unique" selling past. Whether it's a discussion about prospecting, sales talking points, or uncovering value, you'll always hear, "We've tried that before". Let's take a look at the different ways in which companies have been attempting to make sales effective over the last 100 years.

1890-1920: Marketing Engineering Age

The selling limit. During this time, innovative organizations concentrated on identifying sales goals. We knew that sales people had to establish trustful relationships and to be experts on their goods and services. Most specifically, businesses focused on identifying effective sales processes, strategies, and approaches. Around this time, people started to think and write about what the sales process included.

Most specifically, people sought to educate new sales people proactively about the nature of their trade. The bulk of the learning was casual and cantered on teaching people how to sell by example and coaching. Pioneering sales managers made it possible for fellow managers and new salespeople to be tracked by isolating the transaction at a particular moment on why it happened, what happened, and also how to eliminate errors in the future.

Because the sales managers were usually experienced sales people, they could relay tales and share effective techniques for customer interaction. Here are the questions they considered during this era:

- Should we set up a sales incentive program?
- Does the sales training concentrate on creating experts in the field?
- How long should the standard training process take?
- Should the company concentrate on one transaction at a time?

1920-1945: The Consumption Period

This age experienced a revolution in distribution and sales preparation. Before this time, the emphasis was on helping salespeople to identify and close one transaction at a time. Sales teams soon discovered that strategies based on the previous age created several problems.

Teams had trouble expanding their efforts to meet the needs of more people. So, the emphasis was now put on generating sales transactions in a more systematic way. Group leaders and sales coaches had developed new methods of educating sales representatives to build familiarity and recognition of service and products.

In this period, many of the words that we are using today were coined: area, canvassing, sales team, target, and selling cycle. Up until then, most salespeople have trained on the job using self-directed test and trial and error methods or simply by looking at others. Sales managers continued to use written tools like books to teach their sales teams.

The curriculum had been developed to help sales people understand the advantages and benefits of the products, how to deliver it efficiently, and how to close sales, firmly. Comprehensive sales strategies were centered on the importance of innovative product presentations and the practice of overcoming and resolving objections. During this era, the expansion of credit opened up opportunities for explosive sales growth. Here are the questions they considered during this era:

- Who is the best qualified to train new sales members?
- Should we introduce motivational talks, regularly?
- How can we get printed sales training materials?

- Should sales managers assume any mistakes result from their inability to motivate a team?

- How can our business successfully process several transactions at a time?

- Should the sales department rely on "flashy or "functional"?

1945 -1985: The New Abundance Period

Around this time, shortly after World War II, disposable income exploded as customers began seeking more and more luxuries in their lives. Since the advent of mass communication (such as television) and proliferation of print media, the advertiser and marketer's era had finally arrived.

Printed newsletters had become more popular, and more publications had been endorsing the requirements of growing sales organizations. During this time, sales training was aimed at helping salespeople gain attention from the prospective customer and generate interest.

Most sales people were taught the customer incentive hierarchy. Sales preparation covered various styles and specific needs of consumers (i.e., consumer groups, gatekeepers, behaviors, demographics, etc.). Sales teams in this era had access to successful closing strategies and previously documented answers to customer's concerns, doubts and buyer's language.

Emergent technology, such as cell phones and fax machines, had also been equipped, making it easier for sales people to reach new customers. As a result, consumers had faster access to salespersons, to get buy what they needed. Here are the questions they considered during this era:

- Should we design training around the types or industries of our customers?
- Should the sales team continue to support customers after delivery?
- Should training focus extensively on resolving challenges and "canned" responses?
- Should the company concentrate more on the individual sales tasks or the big picture goals?
- Should marketing and sales teams work hand-in-hand?

1985-2005: The Internet Era

The Internet boom was synonymous with the increasing use of computer technology by consumer organizations. When selling processes became well established and had an effect on consumer behavior, companies turned to technology to help speed up the sales cycle and better understand their customers.

Customer relationship management and sales force automation had become a huge requirement. Customer insights and analytical information had become readily available and could streamline the way marketing, sales and service delivery departments worked.

In the sense of sales training, more focus was placed on after-sales service and bundled goods into more comprehensive solutions. Organizations began to educate salespeople about consultative selling practices and how to qualify customers for their solutions.

Sales people had to learn to think on their feet and become problem solvers. Influencing purchasing decisions had become the number one goal of growing organizations.

Sales managers started hiring new talent instead of teaching established sales people, over and over. Training programs began to focus on new recruitment and sign-on incentives, because qualified sales talent became more challenging to find. Scattered teams also made organized sales planning and annual activities more challenging. Here are the questions they considered during this era:

- How do we effectively hire a person with the right skills and personality for the job?

- What exactly should be included in the new hire training?

- What should new vs seasoned sales people be responsible for?

- What should sales managers vs sales people be spending most of their time on?

What Makes the Best Leader for Change?

When market conditions begin to change, you'll find that your company will need to change too. Many organizations are slow at adopting new policies, procedures and processes. The ones that do, usually appoints a change management leader. This is someone who will be responsible for shaping the strategic direction or a change initiative for your organization.

The role does not have to be filled by one person, many organizations even consider appointing a team who is responsible for deciding and documenting the transformation process.

You will ask yourself three questions when assessing possible candidates for this role: Do they have the right approach? Do they have the right knowledge? Or have they learned the skills they need? Let's look at any one of these points of view.

The Wrong Past

Change is really a complex and laborious process that inspires feelings and emotions. Angry or disgruntled team members, competing goals, unexpected problems, or opposition behind the scenes are common daily challenges. A project manager cannot lead their team without patience, dedication and endurance.

The chosen individual must be able to completely commit themselves to see to that the project is completed. An excellent way to do that is to nominate an optimistic and enthusiastic person who is interested in advancing their career within the company.

They will find the obstacles as a unique opportunity for career growth and will be very inspired to succeed. This high potential employee would have a deeper understanding of the organization, an established partnership network, and stronger leadership skills.

As the Chinese term "Ren" explains, when the two strokes that help each other indicate that "knowledge and abilities" have to be balanced with "beliefs and attitudes." An individual with the appropriate knowledge and skills and an inappropriate attitude cannot contribute too much to their company and the company's culture.

The change manager must be ready to stand up for the initiative, even if it means influencing other leaders like you! If they don't believe in the company and their work, they may underestimate the value of their duties and do a poor job. The company must also devote resources; to prioritize this change and continue to be helpful and understanding throughout the transition.

The agent of change must serve as a voice of consciousness and reason. If differences arise in the mid-course, the change manager has an obligation to discuss the problem with the supporters. Otherwise, the project will fail. A successful change agent has this attitude: "My main focus is to make sure this project will succeed, no matter what. The secondary goal is to retain my professional relationship with all executive management and team members."

Adequate Awareness

The change manager of the project should be an accomplished change agent with an overall understanding of what needs to get done. Subject matter expertise also brings prestige and appreciation to the performance and outcome of the change project.

Simply put, the better you understand how the business works, the smoother the transition will be. The chosen person should possess functional knowledge on the sales process, marketing, and the production and delivery of goods and services.

An agent of change must also be possibly the best-connected in the company in addition to having the applicable skills. Active relationships are essential for effective communication with stakeholders, the formation of coalitions, and successful implementation of change.

The Necessary Information

Transition is not as easy as ABC; there is always tremendous pressure on project leadership. A change agent will work under immense instability and uncertainty. They must handle conflicting priorities, different constituencies, and fast deadlines. They are responsible for overseeing the company through many transformation challenges. Therefore, they must have demonstrated the capacity to remain highly successful under extreme pressure.

The agent of change also requires excellent analytical skills, as well as a very coordinated and focused way of thinking and behavior. Sometimes information can be right, or useful, but impossible to defend. When seeking approval from stakeholders, ensure your change agent can provide information that is rational and derived from well-researched sources.

Change managers will need to engage and reassemble processes and structures in new ways. They should have a broad understanding of the effects of what they need to achieve. At the same time, the right change agent must be sufficiently flexible to be able to tackle obstacles and resolve changing priorities. In other words, to face the challenges, a disciplined yet versatile approach is needed.

Having people skills like the ability to relate to others, patience and active listening are imperative to this role. Using the expertise of the team members, the change manager will need to build a strong sense of identity, intention and ownership to achieve results.

The change agent must begin by knowing and accepting opposition as a necessary part of the change process. They will need a great deal of empathy, and excellent listening skills. Most importantly, they must be willing to put themselves in the shoes of others affected by the change.

When change is forced, resistance can be dangerous. Employees are likely to quit, request for a transfer, quarrel, become hostile, or even form a strike. To keep your company from getting into this state, the change manager must be able to communicate at all levels.

Who Makes a Good Change Manager?

Remember that it is never easy to change and that the failure rate is high. I strongly recommend that you take a closer look at your applicants to improve your chances of success. If none of them closely correlates to your needs, it's okay to hire externally. Last but not least, if you find the right person, make sure they can devote 50 % to 100% of their time on the change initiative.

What Is Sales Management?

Sales management could be seen as a part of the marketing mix of the company. This would include the development of promotional strategies, product inventory and pricing, promotional marketing activities, distribution function, and preparation, staff management, training, encouragement, and monitoring of sales personnel to meet the required targets.

Sales management provides aspects to build the sales team, organize sales teams, forecast and plan sales, identify customer's potential, maintain customer information, and create and manage schedules.

The critical functions of the sales management are to provide a clear vision of the operations of direct reports and of the selling activities of the company.

Sales management's essential functions are managing sales structures and territories, such as turnover for critical companies, sales forecasting and reporting, management of the quota, sales representatives' assignments, change implementation, and incentive management, and compensation plans.

The sales management of an organization is strengthened by the active participation of its staff members in internal and external programs, such as meetings or conferences to discuss the matter; training for people in the mode of introduction, learning and transitional periods; as well as seminars, where information exchanges and discussions are held.

These personalized activities allow staff to become more familiar with individual productivity and working in a team. So, your sales processes can be simplified, sales performance is more accurate, sales champions are recruited, and they learn about working motivation methods and mastery of the art of sales, as well as sales coaching, tactics and improvements in strategies.

The job of the sales manager is to give their subordinates the proper environment. This is critical when assessing, challenging, and resolving problems of sales productivity.

To be effective in these respects, a sales director must equip themselves with the methodologies for sales planning and know how to use key performance indicators to control the sales process. In order to increase sales efficiency, the emphasis should be on sales generation rather than on business outcomes.

Sales staff or sales managers are the other aspects of sales management. These are individuals who are appointed on behalf of the organization in a particular territory to solicit business.

A sales representative must identify and address two requirements in order to establish successful sales relationships. These are the psychological needs of the prospect, i.e., questions about what makes them happy; and their prospects needs related to industry, occupation, lifestyle, or hobbies.

Effective sales management also requires an understanding of a customer's future needs. Companies will need to train their sales teams to focus on anticipation so they can continue to improve product and service quality. This research can be conducted by a simple over the phone questionnaire or online survey.

Who Achieves Success in Sales?

Increasing sales performance doesn't mean you need to slash or discount your prices. And sales success isn't judged by who has the highest intelligence. Who really succeeds in sales? The people that practice honesty with each person they come into contact with. There is also no substitution for integrity when it comes to business.

People in sales, whether at the top or bottom should walk and breathe dignity into everything they do. Hire people whose attitudes align with their actions. Great sales people, whether they win the deal or not, lean on their values and principles.

How should you define integrity? I would describe it as adhering, regardless of circumstances or result of such commitments, to strong ethical and moral standards. In other words, credibility is not really a commodity. Plenty of people are using it casually, only when it helps and then throwing it away, if it does not. Consistency is one of the distinctive indicators of real honesty. Hire sales people who are consistent, this will lead to excellence.

Even your sales trainers, must undoubtedly exercise a great deal of dignity, due to the level of influence this position requires. Over the length of their career, they will have observed many people and transactions. As a sales "leader" they need to demonstrate their ability to promote consistency within a sales environment and deliver on strong values and ethics.

Integrity begins by enabling yourself to be responsible privately and publicly for all that you do and say. Indeed, honesty is more about personal responsibility because it is the real responsibility of integrity to lead you every day in your activities and actions.

Things to remember when it comes to improving integrity at your organization:

- Nobody can be forced to work with dignity. It is entirely an internal choice mirrored in external actions.

- It's never too late in the beginning. If you have continued to struggle with integrity in the past, start setting a new course today. Begin to align your company's actions and attitudes in small ways with a substantial ethical and moral standard.

- Accept that every deal cannot be closed because you are unable to compromise your standards.

- The true test of honesty is what your team does when nobody is around and nobody knows what you've have or have not done.

- Learn from those who live and breathe dignity around you. Become a student of your behavior and reactions, not only in the right circumstances, but particularly in difficult circumstances.

- Surround yourself and teams with these types of people as much as you can. Hire team members with the same level of integrity your company embodies.

Whether you're in sales for a short time or for years, you owe it to yourself to reach an integral degree of success. Such success cannot be matched. You will have long-term success, and best of all, it will come in a manner that you will least expect.

CHAPTER 2

The Sales Team Structure

The 4 Core Sales Roles

The first thing you can do to boost your sales and lead generation performance is to focus on filling the right positions at your sales organization.

The four main sales positions

- Prospectors
- Inbound Lead Qualifiers
- Closers
- Customer Success/Account Management

Early-stage companies that are more agile may only need two persons (and sometimes just one person) to start. Mature companies who are high growth oriented and generating a lot of leads will need a separate person to work each stage of the sales funnel.

If you are in an organization that still has its sales staff prospecting for new customers, handling existing customers, and supporting the long-term sales process, you'll profit from hiring individuals for each of these primary roles:

1. Prospector: This job has many titles, but is generally known as a business development rep. Their job is to ensure high growth opportunities for the business. They will likely source new customers by networking, cold calling or re-connecting with dormant accounts. Once they establish rapport about the business and ask to set an appointment for a follow-up call, they are handed over to a lead qualifier.

2. Lead Qualifier: This person will have a discussion with the potential lead that is handed over from the business development team or from marketing. These are the people who will conduct product demos, provide more information and make sure the prospect feels comfortable enough to buy from your company.

3. Closers: This person's job is to follow-up on leads who have been qualified but were not ready to buy immediately. Their job is to convince the prospect to move forward. This person should also be able to jump in and help other team members who lack the skills to close deals.

4. Account Managers: Their job is to stay in touch with current clients and continue to process orders and service their future needs.

Delivering Service Satisfaction

Successful client delivery will continue to fuel growth and customer retention. It's your sales team's job to help consumers obtain more value from the company through hands-on assistance, training, and more. Each person in a sales role should demonstrate the willingness to go above and beyond for their prospects and customers.

The Role of Sales in an Organization

The sales department plays a critical role in the performance of every company. The single, essential function of sales is to bridge the gap between the customer's future needs and the products/services the company offers. Here are the main ways that revenue is influenced by the success of the organization:

Sales Lead Conversions

Sales people are hired to close the gap between consumer expectations and the product or services they need. The sales team should already have an established knowledge of the business through training efforts, and it is their job to close the sale by providing more information and influencing purchasing decisions. When they receive a lead, it's their job to convert it into revenue.

Take car sales, for example. You usually go to a car dealer, knowing that you want a car. The car seller asks typical questions about your personal life, including family size, regular everyday routine, etc. to provide knowledge into the use of the car. You will also include details about various vehicles in the dealership range that match your needs and help you determine which car is the one for you.

Since salespeople connect directly with potential buyers, they have the advantage of collecting personal information that helps them execute their sales pitch and tailor their deals to their audiences. A purchasing decision can usually be made if the seller acts as a caring professional who plans on building a long-term relationship with the prospect.

Referral Business

Sales play a significant role in building consumer loyalty and trust. Trust and reliability are the key reasons a customer wants to recommend your business or write a positive review online of your product or service online, or recommend you to a friend or family member.

Prospects and clients have always appreciated recommendations and reviews, which come from a third party and are perceived to be independent of the seller and, therefore, more credible. Thanks to the popularity and strength of social media and online media, they have a tremendous impact on an organization's credibility today. During a successful sales experience, motivate your customers to recommend a friend or provide positive feedback, this will improve brand recognition and sales revenue.

Customer Retention

Selling is a personal interaction, and a powerful thing, between one human and the other. Never underestimate a link between two people and the potential impact on the reputation of your brand. Excellent sales people are people who not only sell, but also have a lasting impact on the customer. Long-term connections with customers lead to repeat business and word of mouth that improves the popularity of the company.

One of the keys to keeping customers through sales is to track sales. Hosting a post-sales survey or having a quick check-in call is an ideal way to maintain and build a positive relationship and gives the customer an opportunity to comment about their product or service experience.

If the customer has a complaint or problem, it can be addressed quickly and professionally. Unhappy customers too often are quick to complain or simply switch to another provider. It is less expensive to retain customers than to win new ones, so take good care of your existing customers.

The power of sales in an organization's continued success cannot be underestimated. Take advantage of its impact not only on your revenue, but also on brand reputation, long-term retention of customers, and business growth.

Hiring Graduates and Interns for Sales

Currently, it can be a long and drawn out process to find a suitable sales position as a new graduate or intern. Very few companies have established teams with the ability to quickly train them. Since generating sales of prime importance, they often like to recruit people with extensive sales experience.

In fact, if applicants are hired and trained by a reputable company, this will greatly increase their chances of being hired by even more organizations in the future. It's a good idea to hire interns when you have sales projects that you are struggling to get complete, or you'd like to create a pool of qualified applicants in the future.

Before any individual can succeed in sales, they must have the right mindset and a desire to achieve results. These two are the main ingredients, and it would be difficult for applicants to have a productive and successful sales career. That is why many companies set up an internship training program for acquiring the top talent and growth focused graduates.

Setting up a program like this will familiarize the new hires with your company and ensure you are able to hire top-notch sales workers in the future. Regardless of the business field, whether the financial, banking, medical, or IT industries, the experience and knowledge gained from a sales focused company will make a difference.

Companies who hire for intern positions should continually demonstrate their confidence in the candidate's long-term success. When a company has successfully recruited and trained a suitable person for the position, they will typically provide full support and advice to them.

This helps candidates to relax into their new position immediately. It also helps them to start making successful contributions quickly.

Organizing A Team to Quickly Scale

It's impossible to maintain growth and accomplish your business goals without the right processes. You need a solid foundation if you really want to further or scale your sales efforts.

It's not a good idea for sales managers to prioritize a short-term strategy and fast solutions while rejecting the company's long-term needs. Sales teams will always need to fulfill customers' immediate needs in order to meet their sales goals.

Therefore, you need to become strategic to scale your sales team. Rapidly growing sales organizations possess three main characteristics:

- Simple onboarding and training processes
- Effective methods of for generating sales
- Solid framework in place to support growth

The organization's ability to quickly onboard and orient the employee, will not only support the individual, but ultimately profit the organization. A robust induction and integration process will help you to set clear expectations for every new recruit. Good habits and a consistent, high-quality approach with a uniform training program should be established from day one.

If you do not invest in a skills development program for new employees, you will never make the most of hiring them. You will be caught in a continuous cycle of revisiting objectives and revising predictions that reflect slow progress.

A simple, easy-to-learn CRM will quickly assist you, with onboarding new sales team members. New employees need an intuitive sales tool that they can learn in hours, not weeks or months.

Set the right selling targets to boost team motivation and morale from the start. For new salespeople, too many tasks, can feel overwhelming. It's helpful to break down any complex processes and begin with what is manageable, first. You must both trust and inspire your team to achieve their objectives to maintain success in a growing market.

When deciding on an effective sales method, it may feel like a balancing act to find the right level of motivation to keep your people engaged. What works for one team, may not work for the other. One team may be driven by competition, one by commissions, and another by the achievement of team objectives collectively.

As sales managers, it is essential to apply the right amount of pressure to motivate your sales people without going overboard. Especially when the competition is demoralizing for your teams.

Setting the right priorities at a team level will lead your teams to success. Team goals should enable members to work together to share expertise, support each other, and celebrate the progress of individuals and teams.

Team objectives also allow sales managers to easily monitor how the team progresses towards its goals. A CRM system will provide a visual summary that will enable you to compare individual performance and team performance to highlight (and celebrate) strengths and recognize the sales people who encounter disturbances or productivity loss.

Having this level of visibility means you can create a proactive plan to change the course of action if obstacles arise. One way to stop these losses is to start using an action-oriented approach to set goals that the team can reliably achieve.

You cannot completely control the results in sales, but you can control the actions and the inputs in the sales process. If you turn your target into a number of manageable tasks, it's much easier to take action.

Changing your strategy from performance to market-driven sales will help the team regain control of its revenue and keep the members on course throughout the year.

This approach also includes recognition of smaller business goals such as number of upsells or highest average order increase. These objectives will encourage your employees to close the right customers for your company and focus their attention on building customer relations rather than celebrating the biggest deals.

Giving your teams a clear and aligned focus will allow your employees to invest more time in sales. And with the right instruments in place, you can track your success more effectively and continue to refine your selling process.

Strategy will describe the objective and structure will decide your strategy. The correct sales team structure is what works best for your company and salespeople. In this part of the process, a little trial and error are worth going through if it means your business can grow faster in the long term.

When your sales team expands, you'll find that having sales people who are "generalists" will affect your performance. This is not unusual. In a scaling business, a team of 'generalists' will quickly become inefficient. Inconsistencies will emerge, and team members will continue to contend against opportunities, leads, and offers they are incapable of handling. The best thing to do is create sales specialist roles so you can properly delegate work and processes can be streamlined at the organization.

You may start grouping the sales teams into by product or service line, markets, or industries. This helps the teams to concentrate their approach and become real sales experts.

Many sales managers excel by assigning teams for every step in the sales cycle. in every step of their business life. An assembly line approach to sales management will be the most successful way to help your business rapidly scale. Often the sales assembly lines include:

- **The Hunters:** Responsible for identifying and collecting leads to send to the nurturers and pre-qualify the relevant data.

- **The Nurturers:** Responsible for lead qualifications. Typically, the targets are reached, and questions are asked to decide whether they fit the desired client profile.

- **The Closers:** They are responsible for product demonstrations, the handling of complaints, and any steps required encouraging prospects and closing the deal.

- **The Producers:** This team steps in when the deal is closed and focuses on extending the customer's life, reducing churns, and securing more sales.

As each stage of the sales cycle has a particular team, it simplifies processes and makes it easier for each team to report on the outcomes for which it is accountable. It also reduces the complexity of the sales cycle and eases the identification and resolution of obstacles at an early stage.

The strength of your sales team structure must be to build a repeatable and efficient selling process that enables you to scale fast. Do not allow poor structure to stand in the way of your results.

It is essential to build a concrete foundation for your sales teams to grow and multiply in order to maintain momentum. This includes a streamlined and continuous sales cycle, action-oriented team priorities, and a clear team structure. It also requires the right CRM to be found.

Creating a professional sales development plan should help you to achieve your objectives more rapidly and vigorously than ever before, to preserve the growth speed you need and to motivate your teams to strive for greatness and sales success.

Create A Development Plan for Your Sales

Today's sales applicants have more control than ever before over their career opportunities. In a market that currently has a shortage of experienced sales people, countless companies compete for the same talent. This means that it is not as easy to hire and retain workers as it once was. Today's employees expect their employers to invest in them if they invest in their employer.

One of the best ways to improve employers' chances of acquiring and retaining the right talent is through development plans. Each employee must have a personal development plan. A professional development program is a life-long cycle involving the formation, maintenance, and improvement of knowledge or skills in order for employability to continue.

The personal growth process does not have to include regular promotions or pay rises. Your team members, instead, want development so that they can consistently improve their performance and achieve their goals at every stage of their careers.

Employees need their career development plans to align with their development strategy to feel satisfied and involved in the workplace.

Why You Need Development Plans

In today's sales industry, it is difficult to find exceptional talent and it's even harder to keep the staff you have thoroughly involved and committed to your organization. Constant investment in their advancement is one way for companies to help employees achieve their full potential at the same time and to ensure they remain satisfied at work.

A robust development program keeps the talent pipeline complete and gives your organization a valuable retention strategy. Your team leaders will have more opportunities for improving their talents and progressing their careers. Your business also benefits from people with expanded skills, who can give you a breakthrough and cutting edge against the competition. The biggest advantages of development plans are:

1. Prevent staff from stagnating - Employees like to know you'll have a place for them at the organization in the future. Development plans will help them understand that you are committed to providing job enrichment, rotation opportunities and training to help them grow.

2. Improve their knowledge and ability to sell Management teams spend a lot of time training their employees and participating in one-on-one development sessions. They will eventually learn more about their team's strengths and weaknesses. This helps with future delegation decisions and allows leaders to see how their people require support.

In a growing area like sales, having a knowledgeable sales team is crucial. As the industry opens up new trends and possibilities, you will find out which of your staff are ready to adapt. Constantly helping them to improve their knowledge will ensure success in your field and your ability to achieve a competitive advantage.

3. Maintain their commitment and satisfaction Employees who feel "committed" will always achieve their objectives faster and work more efficiently. Offering a professional development plan is one of the best ways to boost an employee's level of commitment.

If the team members feel inspired and supported at work, naturally, they will start to feel more productive. Moreover, as the individuals are going through their growth stages, they feel like their work helps them to reach their goals in life, leading to more happiness.

4. Retention of more talent - The ability to attract and maintain the right talent is one of the most significant benefits of a development plan. While a team of recruitment experts can bring outstanding candidates to your doorstep, you also have to set up an employer brand, which makes it possible for people to embrace your job offer and want to become part of your team.

You will retain more talent and attract future workers through a growth plan that you invest in, ultimately helping them harness their true potential. Your employees should feel as if they get more than a paycheck from you. Workers who learn with the help and genuine support from their leaders begin to demonstrate loyalty to the company. People will stay on-board longer, as a result of the time and money you've invested in their growth plan.

Which strategy is best for career development?

Since each team member comes with a different level of skill sets, it's helpful to design a unique strategy for each person's development. Ultimately, the goal is to establish a plan that would help both the employee and the employer simultaneously.

Empowered and dedicated workers are more inspired and therefore perform better. Career development ensures that managers benefit from a more dedicated team and higher production rates.

When forming a career development strategy, these are the three most important areas to consider:

- Skills enrichment

- On-going job training
- Leadership advancement opportunities

A focused development plan gives salespeople clear guidance on how to advance their careers and build skills. These programs cannot be created off-the-cuff. They must be organized carefully to satisfy the needs of each employee.

What Should Be in a Growth Plan?

No two development plans are the same, because each employee has different weaknesses and strengths to consider. Sales team development plans follow the framework close to that of a standard development plan. For example, the process includes:

- Analysis of facts (where the employee really is)
- Top priorities and sales targets by position
- Recognizing the need for unique skills (what the employee needs to get where they want to be)
- Selecting suitable events to meet the needs of the staff (organization of training or mentoring).

Ways to continue to building an effective development plan for sales team members:

1. Find the market targets

Make sure you understand what the organization requires before you begin to set targets for the team members. Once you understand the goals of your organization, you can begin to identify the skills, competencies, and knowledge needed to achieve your objectives.

If your company is in a phase of expansion, you will probably need leaders to oversee any new workers you recruit in the years to come. These leaders may need to understand new concepts and their relation to your business. This means you need development strategies that provide leadership skills and technology insight.

Development plans save you time recruiting and employing externals by providing you with access to senior talent within your own team. While these plans do not remove the need for a robust recruiting approach, they will allow you to draw on a pool full of potential from your organization.

2. Talk to the team

Once you understand what your business needs are, it is crucial to understand what level of development your employees want.

Don't just assume you understand the aspirations and skills of each and every one of your employees.

One perfect way to get started with your team members to build individual employee growth plans first. This can happen during a face-to-face conversation during the on-boarding process. Ask the employee these questions:

- What are your professional goals, and how do you think we can help you achieve them?
- How do you plan to evaluate your new position?
- What are the challenges in this position you think you will face?

As your employees grow in your business, you can invite them to "keep notes" about areas they feel they are struggling with. During their next performance appraisal, you can talk about their growth plan and any problems or opportunities they have found.

3. Build an action plan

By reviewing the history of your staff and comparing it against your potential expectations, you will be able to create a growth strategy and action plan that aligns with your business goals.

Development plans can be produced in a wide range of formats. Some include formal activities such as training or working with mentors. Other plans include fewer formal experiences such as networking and job shadowing.

Consider which solutions are most important to your team members and whether you need to prepare your staff. For example, will your staff take time away to complete their training? Will there be someone available to cover their workload during training?

4. Succession planning

You can create a succession plan for every role at your company by planning growth plans for your employees. For example, if your top salesperson leaves, you already have someone ready to enter in this position instead of panic and redistribution of your accounts. This person should have a growth plan that was fulfilled through mentoring, coaching, training & development that had already prepared them to hit the ground running.

5. Provide timetables and efficiency metrics

Finally, make sure the workers can see how they are working towards their objectives. It is also beneficial to add a timeline and to celebrate milestones along the way for your team. This is a great way to inspire people when working towards their career goals.

In addition, remember to provide your employees with performance measurements to show how long they have stayed since the beginning of the year or through their development plan. For example, you can highlight the percentage of a course they have completed or show how they have increased their performance over time in a given area. Quick metrics and daily input from supervisors are a helpful way to keep the workers stay on track.

How to Develop Efficient Development Plans

Like any other resource in your organization, if you want to grow your people, you need to invest the right amount of money and time. Without a development plan, your workers can start to stagnate, neglect their goals, and leave your business eventually for someone else that can offer them what they need. Effective career development plans require more than one day of training once annually.

Companies have a number of options to consistently support and nurture their talents. Make sure you build fantastic growth plans:

1. Treat each employee as a person

It's crucial to sit down and discuss your employee's career goals and personal interests. When talking to your team members one-on-one, you can begin to see which development strategies best suit their individual needs. The inspiration and determination you are looking for should not be placing people in a growth plan that does not fulfill their objectives.

You may also find opportunities for your team members to extend their expertise beyond their current role. This will help them successfully pursue other career opportunities at the organization. Cross-training, for example, is an excellent way to enable employees to collaborate more closely with other team members, because they can understand how every aspect of the organization works together to produce results. Efficient development plans should include:

- Having workers examine different duties in certain positions. For example, a digital marketing specialist can see how a sales analyst understands how marketing leads to transactions each day.
- Increasing soft skills and technological talents:

The development of communication and networking skills for employees will help them thrive.

- Knowledge refresh: Skills can quickly disappear in just a matter of months if not actively used in today's fast-moving world. Make sure your employees can refresh their current knowledge and learn new things that improve the way they work.

2. Customize your learning solutions

With so many different team members, it is unlikely that everyone will learn by using the same techniques and strategies. For starters, you can prefer training sessions on your smartphones or study online in your free time. On the other hand, some may feel better with face-to-face education or mentoring.

Find the best learning strategy for every member of your team and give them the flexibility to choose how to improve their skills. A good option could be to implement cross-generational mentoring opportunities. Letting your team members inspire and teach each other will encourage the growth of a robust corporate culture.

3. Recognize and receive reviews

A recognition component is one of the most significant components to a sales development plan. Sufficient information and support are needed to help people grow. If your team members do not feel that you value the extra work they are doing in learning, they will suffer from lack of motivation.

For your employees to develop, positive feedback is essential. If you notice that some team members and others don't perform in their training sessions, you could suggest they try another learning style.

At the same time, make sure your people have received the praise and incentives they deserve when they reach milestones throughout their education. A simple well-done celebration or a team-wide celebration is a perfect opportunity to make sure everyone feels more involved in their growth.

4. Implement new competencies and monitor your staff

Project plans allow you to spend time, energy, and money on your team members. Ensuring the workers work in their positions to generate the highest return on investment.

Set up chances for your employees to use their new skills and receive feedback. This may mean that individual team members are granted extra responsibility so they can use their expertise while it is still new.

Make sure you bring their fresh talent to the workforce:

- Schedule daily meetings to see how they are progressing

- Monitor their progress regularly and encourage their growth
- Seek feedback on how their development plans would be improved or modified.

Who is Responsible for Developing Plans?

To some extent, any team leader or employer is responsible for ensuring that its people have the skills that they need to flourish. Your employees have a big part to play in their own growth.

While managers can plan their employees with fantastic development opportunities, the eagerness and commitment of your people will also dictate the success of your strategies. No matter how much work a business leader puts in, an unmotivated or uninterested employee can't unlock its true potential.

Learning is a Growing Obligation

Finding employees that will stay committed to their development program, isn't always the easiest. Team members who have shared evidence of continually developing their skills in their own spare time is a huge indicator that they really want to learn.

Consider asking questions based on competencies in the interview, such as, *"Tell us about a time when you have invested in additional training to achieve your career goals?"*

With more people focused on learning, developing a corporate culture that promotes continual growth and improvement should go smoothly. This ensures the development process your existing employees experience in your business is enjoyed. Moreover, the future candidates will know you expect them to undertake further education as well.

Using Team Learning

While different people can take different approaches to their education and career development in your business, growth has to feel like a team activity.

Foster open communication so people can tell you what they like and don't like about your training opportunities or even recommend ways to improve their education. Also, remember to celebrate the team's individual achievements.

For example, if one of your salespeople completes a fantastic training course, bring the whole team together for a festive lunch. This is the best way to show your people that their commitment to training is not only good for their future, but also good for the rest of our workforce.

Underestimating Development Plans

Today, most business leaders recognize that development plans are essential for keeping their team members at the "cutting edge." They need the help of their employers to succeed in ever-changing and competitive markets. Career development programs are one of the best ways to improve performance by organizations, which produce 30% higher results.

Development plans give your team members a win-win opportunity to achieve their personal and career goals while giving your company access to additional competences and effectiveness.

The more you invest in development and learning, the more the organization is able to achieve positive results, increase innovation, and enhance employee engagement.

Tips for Building A Sales Focused Organization

Managing transactions is not the same as having a sales strategy or program in place. Most businesses simply restrict their own profits by following a passive selling strategy. Four things can increase businesses' revenues proactively.

1. Create a good distribution network. A sales program encompasses the entire spectrum of sales operations, from selection and prospecting to negotiation and closing. A good system helps you to monitor transactions on the pipeline in real-time, classify the opportunities for high productivity and determine the cost, or look for sales in the most likely locations, based on historical data, in the most efficient ways.

2. Encourage a sales culture. Whoever communicates with people outside the company shapes the expectations of the market. Since expectations shape consumer behavior, expose your sales team to your assumptions of how they should represent the organization when communicating with others in meetings, emails, and other communications. Their position as ambassadors should be part of their job. Encourage a community that seeks to identify and fulfill consumer requirements. Sales will always follow.

3. Introduce the correct sales management. The most excellent sales managers are competitive and efficient. They are also motivating, supportive, system-oriented, and effective communicators. You want the sales managers to do their jobs efficiently with all these values. The top sales people too frequently get promoted to management regardless of how appropriate they are or aren't for their new position.

4. Sell to current and former clients, not just prospects. Like many successful businesses, active companies are to upsell new customers and reconnect with previous customers. Encourage the management and sales teams to concentrate their efforts on current customers' needs and continuously evolving circumstances and to keep ex-customers coming back.

CHAPTER 3

How to Support a Sales Team

Knowing Your Sales Process

Grab a notebook to write down all the actions a buyer needs to take to complete a transaction of your product or service. How many steps are there? How do you take that step, and what does that mean for the customer? And what if you lose a level or skip a step? What do you tell your buyers about this?

So, many businesses don't know their method, they don't know who is responsible for each move, and instead, wonder why the sales department takes too much time to close or finalize a deal.

If nobody knows the process, how can the consumer depend on you to deliver what you said they would deliver? Does the sales manager feel that stuff should be done as promised? Does the company know what the client needs, and does the selling department have the right information and data to qualify them? How can a customer believe someone that doesn't even know what the buying process is?

Teamwork is expected here. No matter how big or small the organization is, there must be a documented sales process of who does what. Once everyone in the business knows what to do, customers will continue to believe that questions will be answered, orders will be delivered and they will be treated as promised.

Where Are the Clients in the Sales Process?

Have you ever made a purchase and became unsure of when you'd actually receive your product? And if you never received it on time or even at all, you probably had a disappointing experience. All customers want is for you to deliver on your promises. If there is a problem, they expect you to fix the issue quickly with minimal to no pain.

Clients are involved from start to finish in the sales process. They are constantly expecting your team to convince them of giving you their business, keep them in the loop and highly informed on product or service delivery expectations. If you are running a dysfunctional operation, you will find yourself wasting time, money and resources trying to resolve things that keep going wrong. Spend time optimizing your sales process. This will ensure things go right, more often.

Who is Responsible for the Sales Process?

After you design your process, the next step is to document them and share it with the entire organization. It is essential for everyone to know the sales mechanisms, thoroughly understand their position, and to be considered accountable. Team members need to know exactly what to do or who to escalate issues to, in order to quickly be resolved.

Everyone in the sales department should understand the procedures that are supposed to take place. Communicate why each step is necessary and what it means if they fail or skip one step.

The process has to be controlled, and the ultimate owner of the process must be present. This may be a vice president of operations, a sales manager, and a project manager. Everyone must be able to control, handle, and make the required improvements in the sales process at any given time.

Why Your Standard Sales Process May No Longer Be Effective

News Flash: Prospective purchasers have become sharper than ever. Since the invention of the Internet, people can now quickly learn about your business and your competition. Most shop savvy customers will go to Google before setting up a call or meet with you. The days are gone from when you came to an introductory meeting and inspired them with your unique business model.

Therefore, what should you do to combat the technical knowledge that the potential consumer has acquired before a call?

Tip1: Give them credit for doing their research and be prepared to address objections.

Tip 2: Try to pivot from the traditional selling cycle you're using. Be willing to negotiate terms to win new business from people who are still "on the fence" about buying.

It's important for your team to concentrate on what "stage" you are in the selling process rather than simply handling objections and moving on. When speaking with prospects, open the discussion around the buyer's key reason(s) to buy and how interested they may be in moving to the next stage.

Feedback is really insightful after the initial pitching stage. Sales teams should always be seeking to excite and delight the customer. This will make them feel comfortable being honest and confirm if they truly believe your solution would be a good fit for their use case.

The sales team will likely have several customers to reach, who are often interested but not verified buyers. Asking clarifying questions will help weed out the people who aren't ready to buy and ensure your sales people can meet their annual goals.

Always stay on top of and measure your current sales performance. Put your money and resources into what makes the greatest impact. If you are interested in doing a large volume of sales, your team cannot waste time chasing or following up with customers who are not ready to buy.

Reasons to Use a CRM System to Manage Sales

To ensure a constant revenue stream from your company, you have to track and sustain a customer base, which includes not only your current customers and prospects, but also a healthy list of potential prospects. It's kind of like watering plants. You need to continuously feed or water the business to keep it rising, or it will get ill and die just like a plant that is not taken care of.

For companies who plan to grow, I suggest the use of a CRM system. There are still companies today running their entire business off of an excel spreadsheet. This is how they actually monitor their buyers and prospects. I believe deeply in the use of processes and technologies to maximize the performance of a business' everyday sales management.

For many people who do not understand, CRM stands for customer relationship management. CRM solutions can improve customer loyalty, maximize efficiency, and raise profitability. Here are the top reasons a CRM should be used:

1. Sales and marketing systems should be streamlined and standardized.
2. You can store and update contact records, events, emails, etc. by having the same up-to-date or live client details and opportunities within a team environment.
3. Programming of events, memoranda, and schedule sharing for sales teams.
4. Increased prospects for cross and up-selling.
5. Separate connections and groups by different standards (A,B,C, customers per company, sector, preferences, etc.) that will allow for better classification and targeting of customers.
6. Customer service is strengthened by loyalty and retention. When you track your events and get valuable information about your clients and their companies, it will encourage you to be constructive rather than reactive about your company.
7. Increased productivity overall. They usually come equipped with fantastic sales and lead generation tools.

I would suggest using free trials to find out which CRM program is right for your company.

Boosting Sales Through Business Marketing and Technology

Can the sales team actually create stronger consumer relationships? Will your sales team draw consumers' attention? If not, a marketing strategy needs to be created or updated to match the demands and stay abreast of emerging industry patterns.

Marketing and promotions are the practice of studying the market to offer goods and services to prospects in-need and ultimately drive sales. Your marketing strategy should define the desires of customers, their attitudes, beliefs, how you will satisfy them, as well as build customer satisfaction, and continue to develop relationships.

It incorporates delivery, advertising, product creation, product marketing, advertising, and management of customer relations. This also positions name, product blend, and efficient distribution of capital and funds. A good strategic plan will also test a product, service, or brand's market superiority in comparison to its favorable offerings.

Make sure you have built a successful marketing campaign based upon its relevance to your target market. Since the emergence of technological advancement, buyers' tastes have evolved, and industry patterns have changed. Companies need to adapt their marketing strategy and approach to match consumers' desires, lifestyles, and behavior.

Organizations should be everywhere their potential customers are. With modern day technology you can easily place your ads on your customer's favorite blogs, videos, social networks, online magazines, digital signage and more. Always plan to position your ads in high trafficked areas whether online or offline.

Organizations should use innovative communication campaigns and the best technologies available to draw consumers. You can touch millions of potential clients with a creative, attention grabbing campaign. Seeing that the success of a company primarily relies on the quality of services and goods sold, a successful marketing plan is also necessary.

Company marketing advantages:

- • Increases brand awareness in the marketplace
- • Generates consumer loyalty and retention
- • Helps to identify prospects for the sales team
- • Provides product knowledge to customers for pre-sales

- • Establishes potential partnerships to benefit brands
- • Improves overall trust and market perception
- • Clarifies the quality of goods and services offered

Sales Training - How Much and How Often?

Managers and team members alike, frequently ask the question, "How long and how often do I get sales training?" Here are also some valuable tips for sales managers who want to learn how much and how long to train their team:

Evaluate the staff before training: Most sales teams represent a mixture of expertise and creativity within their salespeople. A successful sales manager assesses the team's strengths and deficiencies. The review must cover those who are new to the organization and those who have already been fully trained.

The methods and duration of sales training can ultimately be dictated by the assessment performance. The sales manager should customize their training plans to suit the expectations of their company as a whole and for individual sales people.

Defining training results: Sales preparation may be geared towards the technological selling cycle, specialized sales experience, or product or service awareness. The purpose of training is, in most situations, motivational, and expected to produce a positive change in the organization.

Managers will use the outcomes of the tests to perform tailored preparation to mitigate the general shortcomings of the sales staff. They should also be targeted to those who need specific skills or knowledge.

Make sure everybody is educated in the fundamentals: The whole selling team needs to be proficient in the basics. Secondly, they need to understand the fundamental elements of a sales cycle. These include: prospecting, recognition of requirements, feature-benefit approaches, and closing.

Finally, sometimes even the fundamentals require some modifications so that it fits the selling culture and matches the nature of your business. Much as a professional baseball team needs spring or pre-season sessions, selling teams need basic training from time to time for everyone as a refresh. Use the more experienced sales people to hold group sessions or improve basic training.

So, the answer to the question, "how many and how long" depends on the selling team's expertise and results. In some instances, a workshop for one or two days may be helpful, even though it eliminates workers from production. Hopefully, average sales results can be increased by enhancing specific capabilities of each and every team member.

For other situations, shorter training sessions may be required. You can start with weekly or monthly sales sessions. This form of education can also be carried out through video chat or webinars performed by sales managers or other professional sales staff.

In the end, the decision on how much and how long is usually determined by the sales director or senior sales manager. Always remember, the best employees are the ones that are the most trained.

Required Marketing & Sales Support Materials

Today, not having enough sales support materials is a top concern for decision makers and sales focused organizations. A sales team will need to focus on what they do best, which is selling! Make sure your team is equipped with brochures, presentations, and pdfs that contain the most important information about your product/service or brand.

If you expect them to close deals faster and win new business. You will need to invest in high-quality literature that makes the sales process easier and more effective. Here is a list of other marketing assets that will help smooth out the sales process:

Website: With globalization today, getting a website is imperative for any company. Luckily, several websites provide hosting free of charge. You will need to register a domain name, buy hosting and get a website designed. The platform you choose does not have to be complex. But it must contain all the details you need about your business and how to contact your sales team.

Case Studies: Do you want to convert leads into customers and move the sales process along? A case study demonstrates that you know what you're talking about and you've been able to provide valuable solutions to clients in the past.

Brochures: These are great to have on hand at trade shows and even around the office. Brochures are an effective and simple marketing tool that help introduce your company's products and services.

Banner Ads: If you plan to advertise on the web, banner ads are a MUST. These little babies generate a big chunk of revenue for growing businesses.

Proposals: If you plan on writing up special offers for your customers, you'll need a branded proposal. You can easily boost your credibility with a high-quality business proposal template.

Presentations / Slide Decks: Got a big presentation coming up? You'll need a custom branded slide deck to not only look professional, but reduce friction when it comes time for your prospects to make a buying decision.

Product Catalogs & Spec Sheets: Customers will often have a lot of specific questions about your products or services...and much of it can be quickly answered by sending them a catalog or spec sheet. This is another great tool that helps you close sales faster.

Email Templates: For the sake of time and money, you should always have a pack of email templates ready to go for your brand communications. Whether that is just header & footer graphics or an automated sales script. Email templates allow your team to be efficient when trying to sell or communicate important updates.

Landing Pages: These make it easy for people to buy your products, because the page has only one specific goal. It removes all the distractions and suggests that the customer either buy now, or opt-in for more information. You should always have at least 3-5 landing pages to promote your most valuable offers.

Videos: These are a triple threat! It's a great way to drive traffic, brand awareness and improve SEO. Always have a least one video that introduces your company and educates the consumers on what exactly you do.

Brand Guidelines: For those of you who are unfamiliar with the brand guidelines document. This piece of collateral governs your brand's designs, and the look and feel of all of your marketing materials. This will dictate how your logo should and shouldn't be displayed, what tone of voice you should and shouldn't use in social media, how your email signatures should look, it'll outline your vision and mission statements as well as standardize your key messaging. This is super important to have to ensure brand consistency and to make sure everyone in the organization is on the same page.

Why Every Business Must Have Collaboration Tools

Business coordination tools enable an organization to be very successful. An organization will streamline its processes and discover opportunities to cut costs by using powerful methods of collaboration. These tools are not only helpful to companies who want to work with other likeminded businesses', but are also crucial to the management of internal workflows. When you have these tools, every enterprise is strengthened, and the faster an organization has the tools, the better.

1. Keep workers focused

Fostering a culture of teamwork is one of the hardest jobs for bosses or business owners. Collaboration tools, however, makes this operation a breeze. These tools enable a worker and a manager (or business owner) to communicate at critical times. It makes it easier for the team to navigate and operate efficiently and effectively through the system. There is no need to work slowly. If an employee needs consent or assistance, their manager (or boss if the business owner is the boss) only needs a few key points. It helps the worker to stay focused and concentrate on active tasks all the time.

2. Lines of communication become open

Communication channels are continually open between the owner, management, and employee. More specifically, these channels of contact are accessible but not distractive. The only thing a business owner (manager or employee) has to do to network with their colleagues is to check their collaboration tools rather than ringing phone lines. These tools and techniques help people to focus on what they do best and they do not have to remove themselves from their day to day workload.

One of the main issues with managing a sales team is that some bosses continue to bother workers while they are busy. Instead of this continually happening all day long, the individual can relax as they can select when to respond rather than when a question immediately arrives in the workplace. This form of working triage allows the person to do more than they can instead of focusing on what they shouldn't do.

3. Sharing files helps you to be quicker on your feet

Most sales staff work on a job where they must collaborate with other employees or employees of another organization. The best way to handle the process is to use a sharing tool to ensure everybody has the current updates on sales support materials or email notes. Sales transactions can be completed quicker and with fewer mistakes.

Finally, any business that needs to speed up its workflow, get rid of mistakes in its product, and communicate more quickly should use useful tools for collaboration. These tools are essential to any business that wants to compete and stay relevant. A business that will grow further than its rivals is a corporation that can ultimately conquer its niches. If every organization wants to become the industry leader in its niche, having the best business sales tools and resources are a must.

Competitive Intelligence - Discover the Competitors Business Strategy

Do you know about your competition, their sales, and their weaknesses? If you need sales insight on how well your competitors are doing, you'll need to invest in a strategic sales intelligence software (CI). Results are not impossible to achieve and will, in turn, be a vital component of your organization's success.

What is Competitive Intelligence?

The Competitive Intelligence Professionals Association describes CI as "a structured and ethical project, which gathers, analyses, and administers external intelligence that can affect the strategies, actions, and activities of the business." You can get intelligence on the most profitable and related companies, future consumers, and developments in the marketplace. Having intelligence on your side will help you make wise strategic decisions moving forward.

Know Your Competitors

Competitive knowledge involves reading between the lines, but a lot of potentially valuable information can be quickly retrieved from the Internet. With sales intelligence software, you can uncover content, website ranking, marketing assets, statistics, keywords, sales and revenue information, past and current client data and more.

Know Your Potential Clients

A company could also use the information to make better decisions about new customers. You can also look at the state tax reports, SEC registration of the firm, see website files, and search for lawsuits and settlements relating to the company. You'll get an understanding of your needs and what the team feels about them.

When a corporation has kept the same legal counsel for the last decade, it might not be a wise position to bring resources into the operation. But, if this current organization needs a new CEO, then they should search for a different company. If you see an individual business change law firms across the seasons, it may be too much of a burden. You will discover all this knowledge through strategic intelligence.

Stand by Ethical Principles

The only thing that is not immoral is strategic intelligence. It's not unethical hacking. Much of the knowledge a law firm wants to know is freely accessible. What is not readily available on the web will also be identified by actually making a few phone calls and answering questions from the right people.

Several prominent orgnizations have CI workplace consultants, but the regulatory sector is reluctant to continue. This is presumably because CI research is typically expensive for consumers and has to be budgeted elsewhere. However, the payoff can be massive, so it may be worth applying strategic intelligence to the sales strategy of the company.

CHAPTER 4

Developing Sales Leaders to Improve Results

Four Famous Issues and Solutions for Performance

Sales efficiency is the foundation of success for every company. A sales team operates best with consistent direction and inclusion. Companies can become much more competitive when they align sales with marketing. Integration among departments usually depends on the company's business strategy and sales strategy. Usually B2B's selling approach requires less cross-departmental coordination than B2C's. So, how well your sales team performs largely can depend on their ability to communicate goals and objectives with the marketing department, who is essentially responsible for generating sales leads.

Poor sales team performance can also be a result of bad organizational design and management, siloed functions, closed corporate communications, and unbalanced rewards.

Common Sales Performance Issues

1. Design and management of the company

If a company has a robust recruitment and on-boarding program that is designed to full train, equip and support the sales team, you"ll find that sales performance is likely to increase. If the orientation trainer doesn't have a good understanding of the sales team's mission, company vision or requirements of the job, your sales team members will be set up for failure.

This dilemma can be reduced by consistent company training and meetings to refresh the team on your mission and goals. You should also provide them with a summary of future plans (three months, six months, one year, etc.), matched with guidance and goals. Some selling teams complain that they are not able to sell because of uncertainty and lack direction. So, moving forward, concentrate on coaching, mentorship, and direction throughout the entire career of each team member.

2. Siloed functions

The role of a modern-day sales team has drastically changed. Gone are the days when they had only one function and didn't need to collaborate with others. It's important for every company to create a unified view of team collaboration, because it has a huge impact on sales. The silo mentality starts with management. Leadership must provide an environment that supports everyone to work toward their common goals. Implementing a CRM system will help your team train, educate and work together. The more they are able to lean on each other for support, the higher their sales performance will be.

3. Closed corporate communications

Although this is not just a sales team problem, poor communication from the top level down can cause significant bottlenecks in the sales pipelines. This problem is triggered by leadership's inability to communicate issues, changes or new company initiatives. This will cause a misunderstanding of the sales team's actual responsibilities combined with uncertainty about who to contact if priorities have changed or an issue arrives.

One standard solution is to standardize the way changes or priorities are communicated with the team. Corporate leaders should have one unified method that is dedicated to communicating updates. Most corporations appoint one specific leader to rally up the team and share details.

Others use email to facilitate communication amongst the team. If your organization doesn't have a standard process for sending and receiving communication, you'll find the sales team's performance will drastically drop.

4. Imbalanced system of rewards

When the sales incentive program isn't balanced, your team members will suffer from poor morality and frustration. Therefore, the future production of revenue cannot be strengthened without fixing this disparity. Each member of the sales team wants to feel motivated to perform, but most importantly the system of rewards needs to be fair and setup so that everyone gets an equal share of success.

Traits of a Great Sales Team

Ever wanted to know why specific teams performed so well? They seem to be magnets for generating new customers on demand. Over the course of my career, I was happy to have worked with many great, high performance sales organizations. Not only did I learn about the characteristics of these high performers, but also about the ideal environment that is required for them to thrive. Here are a few features I found in the super sales team DNA:

1. Energy flow: Teams that tend to excel at generating sales, are explosive with energy. Teams that stick together and evolve are often associated with this strength. Over time, they'll find significant similarities and can call on each other's expertise. This energy match lets them focus on the job and really get down to business.

2. Stability: High performance teams understand when they've gained traction and are not unreasonably worried about their position within the organization. They know their strengths; they have faith in their leadership and compensation. Because of this, many of them are comfortable with leaning on each other to help close deals.

3. Resilience: I haven't yet encountered a single sales person who hasn't had a pressured conversation during their career. Whether from management or a potential customer, for many, it's hard to keep calm and crush your goals. High performance teams learn to cope with this by becoming resilient to the day-to-day, common pressures that come with the job. They tend to balance the workload amongst the team, participate in active listening and remain positive.

4. Competitiveness: Having a competitive spirit is one of the pillars of self-improvement. High performing teams want it all and are willing to do the work to get it. Companies that nurture these *'super teams'* are focused on recognition and retention.

How to Decide on Your Sales Training Initiatives

Sales training programs can waste time, energy and resources if not properly thought out and planned. If you're looking to positively impact the organization with your training, place a crucial emphasis on these long-term outcomes:

1. Adaptation and significance

There are several methodologies used to boost sales in a business. Maybe you have either applied or been exposed to some of the tried and tested sales strategies. In order to make the training experience successful, you need to determine how well the current sales procedures, training content and tools your organization offers can be adopted. If any of these items haven't been successful in the past or slowed down the organization, it doesn't make sense to train the workforce to adopt them.

Each time you plan a sales training, evaluate the materials and information that needs to be conveyed, and measure the significance or impact it could potentially have towards increasing revenue.

2. Delivery

People learn in different ways and in today's world, training options are endless. Some organizations decide to deliver training online, in-person at meetings, via self-paced courses or webinars or through a one-on-one coaching program. Whichever you consider, be prepared to choose a technique that increases motivation and supports changed selling behavior.

3. Reinforcement and implementation of post-event

So many sales organizations are spending thousands of dollars flying in everyone, and spending a couple of days teaching them on the latest sales techniques. The energy and excitement are there, but then everyone goes home and it's back to business as usual.

Sales reps and managers quickly return to their old ways. And everything they learned quickly jumps out the window. Don't make that mistake. Begin mapping out your sales training program with the end in mind. What do you want them to remember? What will be the key takeaways and how will you get it to stick? Allow yourself ample amount of time to consider these questions and design a training program that will be results oriented and produce the best results.

Using Experienced Sales Team to Coach Newbies

Sales managers and senior sales reps are essential to a company's performance and growth. Consistent coaching helps to not only retain staff, but to enhance results, develop skills, and pass on knowledge. In addition to these benefits, teaching others is a meaningful way to improve and share the learning experience.

Leaders who mentor workers will build a much more skilled and flexible workforce, who will contribute to a more stable, growing enterprise. Throughout their sales career, some people may need much more handholding than others. Never be afraid to pair your experienced team members with the newbies in order to keep them on the right track. You can never go wrong with this strategy.

How to Train Workers at Different Levels

With each member of your team, it's best to diversify your coaching style. Transformational, mindfulness and performance-based coaching is amongst the most popular strategies used today. There are five stages of employee success, and each one requires a different coaching strategy to effectively train:

1. The Novices

Novices are in the process of "gaining experience." They must be taught and constructively corrected. If you have confidence in the people you have employed, they probably won't have to stay too long at this point. Be very aware of your own organization's micromanagement patterns – you don't want to keep an employee out of growing to the next step!

2. The Doers

When novices start to understand and practice, they move up to the Doer level. They haven't perfected the job yet, so a lot of "foundational" coaching is still going on. Yet, they do a good job and contribute to the team. There are also many ways to foster better behavior and applaud Doers for their positive performance.

3: The Performers

When the doers begin to perform a role according to expectations, they become performers. They are now doing actual work and carrying their full load. And they do the job as it should be. There is a lot less "directional" coaching for performers, if any. Feedback is still available, and primarily aimed at identifying opportunities and enhancing outcomes that do not meet expectations.

4: The Masters

Experienced performers grow and enter into the Master's level. Not only can they execute tasks to expectations at this stage, but they can also do so effectively and efficiently. In fact, they understand well enough what should be done that they can instruct and train others on the job.

5: The Experts

Experts are essential team members who can become pioneers of the frontline sales team. Experts don't require much guidance – they are incredibly autonomous. If anything, they will have been promoted to a leadership role at the organization. Experts don't need a lot of attention and affirmation to remain motivated.

Executive and Leadership Coaching Tips

Now that we have worked through the various levels of success that your sales workforce can reach – here are a few helpful tips! These work for all five levels and will motivate you to hold a more mutually beneficial coaching session and boost the overall success of your team!

1. Ask questions about feedback

Open-ended directing questions lead to detailed and concise responses. Which leads to more successful coaching discussions. It's better if you develop good relationships with your workers as a boss or leader. This will allow you to assess whether your workers are actually interested in the work they do. You'll find that many have the potential to learn and improve, and want to know honest feedback on how well they are performing.

Feedback also plays a part in emotional intelligence and communication skills. Managers should lead conversations by listening carefully, not just by giving instructions. Employees learn and evolve the most when feedback is revealed.

2. Learn the criticism vs praise ratio

Good coaching requires a combination of criticism and praise. When the coaching discussions are based solely on what doesn't work, which is not inspiring, it's demoralizing. When a less than positive outcome occurs, feel free to provide constructive criticism to your team and honest feedback on where they could have done better. Employees also like to be remembered. So, keep in mind, praise will help enable them to stay motivated and sell more. When things are going right, they want to know that it won't just go unseen or unheard.

3. Develop relationships with your people

The sales team wants to be able to trust their coach. As a sales leader, your role is to develop individual relationships with employees that will enhance results. The staff will probably have a lot of information, questions, and feedback. It is essential for them to know that their coach will listen carefully to what they have to say and allow them to express their views.

Some salespeople will have no trouble communicating, and others will need a lot of support before they freely express an opinion with you. Always make your team feel comfortable sharing their views and opinions without there being a great debate.

4. Understand their opinion

As you mentor workers to boost their efficiency and motivation, addressing problems other than your own will allow you to see the progress and outcomes you want. Everybody has a variety of motives, interests, and behaviors. Be prepared to customize your coaching interactions in order to work better with your team. Try and take a step back and understand their "why" and how a situation appears to them.

5. Explain the next steps

Coaching a sales team is intended to generate improvements and outcomes, so make sure you clearly identify what needs to happen next. It ensures you and your employee meet the standards, as well as land on the same page.

The next steps should be mutually decided – address the realistic expectations considering their workload and the nature of the changes being made. At the end of every coaching session, both parties should have a clear understanding of the next steps and should follow through to make changes and improvements.

6. Engage in continuous learning

Managers and sales coach's alike need to continually develop their own abilities and knowledge. If you don't always know, why should your staff? Lead by example and your team will follow.

If you show up like you're not interested (why should they?) Most sales organizations are in a constant cycle of growth. Show your workers that you not only want them to do better, but that you are personally involved in their work, their successes, and their professional achievement.

Reserving Quality Time to Review Performance

Managing your time effectively helps you to work more efficiently and do more to advance the fundamental goals of the business. As a leader, it is essential to use your time to fulfill your many duties and responsibilities. In order to start making changes at the organization, the first step is to reserve time to review your team's performance.

This time should be used to explore missed or achieved goals, employee's conduct, dependability and responsiveness to the team's overall mission. A performance review isn't required daily or even weekly. Most organizations allocated 30 minutes to each employee on a monthly, quarterly or yearly basis to discuss next steps.

Quality performance review activities are the cornerstone of a company's success. Here's a list of questions to ask each team member when evaluating their performance:

- What are you doing at the moment to help you achieve your goals?
- What was your deadline for the goal to be completed?
- How many hours did it take for you to complete the project, task, or goal?

- Were you able to successfully complete or achieve your goals?
- If you were not able to meet your goals, what do you think was standing in your way?

Sales Goals and Objectives

All actions that don't help us achieve our goals are a waste of time. Sometimes goals can be too large to aim for "all at once". After having a discussion during the performance review, decide if the sales person's goals should be split or divided into smaller steps. Breaking them down may help them accomplish their goals much faster. Planning and setting daily targets will make your team's time management and the sales process more efficient.

- **Set goals once a day**: Either first in the morning, or the next day, and the last thing before going home. Set the goals every day and one at a time, taking into account what you want to achieve before the end of the week.
- **Specific daily targets should be identified.** Which should include where, when, and with whom?
- **Routine goals should be met.** Make it realistic and fair. There should be an excellent opportunity to do it.

- **The target should be mutually established.** If others are involved. It doesn't have to be complicated. For example, state, "then we accept that we will have agreed on the following four questions at the end of this meeting."

- **Active goals should be observable.** While you may not want to always log your progress to your target, the point is if you're going to, you will.

- **The best use of your time** every day is to reach your daily goals this morning (or by the last evening).

Train your team to stop wasting time on less important things. They should be highly focused and concentrated on high priority activities that generate sales results.

How to Determine Sales Potential

Is it possible to actually improve sales? Of course, it is! There are four quantifiable steps that can be used by any manager to discover secret opportunities and improve the end result:

1. Daily sales volume. Understanding this metric will help you assess where you currently stand and where you can start to add-on and create strategies to sell more often.

2. Penetration of the market. If you've been successful selling your products and services to a certain market, you want to explore expanding into new markets to sell more.

3. Territory restructuring. Do you have underperforming territories? It may be time to re-align team members to increase sales performance or design a new sales strategy to increase revenue from those doing poorly.

4. Competitive research. Are your top competitors in a similar situation or are they growing? If so, you probably need to determine if you're dealing with an industry related issue or an internal one.

What Should Be Discussed in Your Training Program

The value of staff training is clear; and effective sales managers know that staff training is a direct means of preventing poor sales performance. In order to improve the quality of work and level of care your people put into their job, training should be a priority for the organization.

However, many organizations are unsure what elements of employee training should be implemented, and what information the employee should reasonably anticipate. Here are the key points to be discussed in a sales training and the necessary information that an employee should learn.

1. Organizational practices and procedures

The organization's practices and procedures will be one of the first things an employee learns. Most companies actually send workers home with a policy manual and expect them to read it themselves.

The best course of action is a straightforward direction, which specifies precisely what the employee is supposed to do. This prevents staff from misunderstanding or not being aware of such policies. The following processes and practices are the ones the employees need to information on:

- Overtime practices
- Working hours planned
- The best way to treat colleagues
- Timeliness requirements
- The best way to deal with a dispute
- Use of corporate assets
- Team structure, key contacts

2. Abuse at work and sexual assault

Abuse and intimidation in the workplace are a significant concern for risk managers. The business could have significant consequences if it does not clearly state what is expected of employees in regards to how to respond to harassment, and the discipline associated with harassment.

Employees need to know the right route to settle a complaint if they feel threatened. They should also be assured that their argument does not have a negative effect on their employment status with the organization. Training on abuse and sexual assault in the workplace will address these main issues:

- Which acts constitute abuse and harassment?
- How aggressive or abuse issues may be identified
- How to respond to the abuse or harassment you have suffered
- The different forms of abuse and harassment
- What to do if you experience abuse or workplace harassment
- Who to communicate with about the situation

3. Control and tracking

While training for employees is generally based on supervised workers, all the supervisors and managers should be adequately trained to ensure success. A lack of preparation for managers and supervisors can have a detrimental impact on the chain of command and can affect all supervised workers down the line.

Those in authority roles must be aware of what is expected of them and how they will respond in such circumstances. Ensuring proper supervision of workers is essential to organizational performance. Management and supervisors should be qualified in knowing the following:

- Rules and procedures to be practiced by staff
- Forms of discipline that are acceptable (and not) for employees
- How to mitigate organizational disputes
- What to do in emergencies (e.g., earthquakes, or fires)
- The protocols that workers are supposed to follow
- How to deal with abusive or sexual assault situations

4. Global Capital

Every employee should understand that internal management ends at a level of external assistance. Organizations providing benefits should review them with their workers in advance so that no complications arise later.

Companies should also provide a brief overview of any benefits or partner programs they partake in. Which could be any of the following topics:

- Dental plans
- Pension programs
- Health and well-being benefits
- Education reimbursement benefits

Executing a comprehensive training program is just one of the easiest and most effective ways in which companies are lowering their risk and increasing their profitability.

CHAPTER 5

Ways to Keep the Sales Team Happy

Open Communication in Sales Management

Sales management relates to the art of achieving revenue goals by successful budgeting and proper preparation within a defined timespan. Sales management helps managers to negotiate deals for the company and ultimately receive profits for it.

Your team's ability to keep in contact plays a significant role in the sales generation process. Communication is the foundation of sales management, without it, no clear agreements can be reached. Sales staff and consumers, as well as sales managers, should be inclined to frequent interactions.

Communication Between Sales Specialists and Potential Customers

Customers now more than ever are frustrated by confusing advertising terminologies and jargons. It is crucial that they understand what you are selling so that they can eventually buy it. Train your team to keep their sales pitch clear and accurate. All members of the sales team must be aware of the features and benefits of what you sell. And must be able to convey and connect that back to the customer's pain points.

Your sales professionals should also be aware of the tone of their voice. They shouldn't be too loud or too quiet, be respectful, and be kind. It's important that customers can hear them clearly and never feel disrespected. These key points should be shared with members of your sales team:

- Wait your turn. Let the customer speak first
- Don't play with language
- Don't play with words
- Make clear value statements
- Don't make fake promises
- Be transparent about the offers
- Your job is to serve, not to judge

Make Sure the Presentation is Impressive

When presenting information to prospects, make sure you team members are not chewing or eating anything whilst on the phone or in-person meeting. It will come off unprofessional and leave a bad impression in the prospects mind.

Their key to making an impressive presentation is to really understand the customers' desires and needs, in order to recommend the right solution. During this time, they may ask a lot of questions to help determine if you are the right choice. Make sure your team is prepared to answer them, as well as remain patient and calm during the process.

Communication Between the Sales Team

In order to make sure your team stays happy; the sales manager must collaborate on an open forum. They will be expecting the leadership to encourage everyone to participate and make constructive suggestions.

Transparency between management and sales professionals must be upheld at all times. Sales representatives should be made well aware of their priorities and rewards from the start to prevent misunderstandings later.

Management should ensure that the goals are practical and achievable. All members should be kept in the loop and receive the same information. You should not interact individually with individuals in locked rooms. It sends a misleading message.

Team members want to feel free to express their opinions and take part in the organization's decision-making process. It's leadership's role to foster an environment where they feel comfortable doing so. When they feel empowered, they will be more inclined to establish good partnerships with future customers and sell more.

Lead Distribution for Sales Teams

Today, most sales focused organizations are trying their very best to be fair with lead disbursement. The problem is deciding whether to distribute them based on selling capacity, expertise or by sales performance?

Every day, sales managers encounter this dilemma as new leads are generated. They struggle to decide on how to delegate new leads to the right representative quickly. Through the use of complex algorithms, lead delivery methods have increased, and the sales process has become more sophisticated.

By matching leads to representatives, you increase the likelihood that a rep has the necessary details to close the deal. When you segment your leads by sector, account size, or annual revenue, the productivity of your sales team can significantly improve. To understand how the lead delivery process works, two major considerations have to be taken into account; speed and reliability.

Speed

Many sellers understand that pace matters instinctively. Leads can be fickle, so it sometimes takes quick action to catch their attention. For example, online leads can go cold in just 90 minutes.

Compatibility

Compatibility refers to the relationship between the knowledge, needs and specifications of the rep. High consistency ensures that the sales representative assigned to each lead has all the relevant details and expertise to validate this account and to convert it into a sale.

Methods of Lead Distribution

Over recent years, corporate distribution stacks have grown tremendously. New electronic delivery systems have forced manual delivery slowly to the side. Although most companies concentrate mainly on automated methods of the lead distribution, manual lead distribution is a great choice for those who are starting on a smaller scale. The most popular lead distribution methods are:

- • Manual distribution
- • Pull-based distribution
- • Push-based distribution

- • Hybrid distribution

Choosing the Best Lead Distribution Method

It may seem challenging to pick one of the many lead distribution methods. Nevertheless, the "right" approach depends entirely on the priorities, culture, and selling process of your company.

I suggest the selection process be started by addressing this question: Do I wish to maximize speed or compatibility? The Pull-based forms of lead delivery work to improve response times. Push-based distribution method matches team members with leads based upon who is "top producer". It's not uncommon for people to combine pull and push methods to yield better results.

In the end, what works for the team depends on the right approach. The approach you choose must ultimately allow your sales team to react quickly and efficiently to close deals. Remember to keep testing and optimizing, as you scale. What works with two representatives will not necessarily work with twenty.

Rewards for Good Selling Behavior

Sales incentives are an effective way to inspire employees. Apply these five best practices to improve the sales team's level of happiness and sustain high efficiency.

Being able to effectively motivate sales teams is a challenge facing most executives. Sales rewards are benefits, promotions, and other resources that inspire members that enhance their results. In tandem with your incentive package, you can motivate sales teams to boost efficiency and sustain high quota efficiency.

There are several ways to use sales rewards to promote success, and you should keep the following factors in mind when establishing or committing to deliver rewards to your team.

- Avoid creating a complex comp program
- Make the path to promotion clear
- Create bonus opportunities that are valuable
- Set simple deadlines
- Make the bonuses attractive
- Set goals that are practical and achievable
- Reward high performance
- Include non-cash rewards in your plan

- Create a rule-based compensation structure
- Introduce smaller rewards for participation

The aim is to build sales incentives around the idea of intrinsic motivators too, if possible. In this way, you do not only give your workers a reward for excellent performance; you affirm and inspire a sense of confidence that drives them to succeed every day.

While it is doubtful that you will be able to meet everyone's individual needs, the more you know your team members, the more you will inspire and reward representatives in a way that connects for your team. Tap into what drives your individual representatives, and you will inspire success.

Paying Commissions on Time

Sales people are intelligent. They are fully aware of the value of achieving their sales targets, and will also be reviewing the sales reports. Sometimes the sales records do not show accurate sales statistics, or a sale could have been credited to the wrong team member.

If a reporting mistake like this happens and commission data is incorrectly calculated, you'll need to quickly reconcile the situation and correct the errors. Mistakes can occur from time to time from either end. Perhaps the customer's check was not signed, or someone made a mistake when logging in the sales. There are endless chances for error.

People want to feel as if they can rely on the companies they work for, especially when it comes down to getting paid on time. No one likes to experience continuous "hiccups" that force them to get paid at the end of next month's salary.

It's important for leadership to pay attention to what's going on, stay on top of the numbers and make sure people get paid on time.

Opportunity for Bonuses

Bonus pay is extra remuneration provided to an employee in addition to their daily salary, which is used as a thank-you to workers or a team for accomplishing essential goals for many companies. Reward pay is often provided to boost the ethos, morale, and efficiency of workers. If an organization adds performance incentives, it may inspire workers to achieve their targets, which in turn helps the company achieve its goals.

What Kind of Bonuses are There?

The incentives may be contingent or non-discretionary. They may be paid out as the company deems fit or may be mentioned in a contract of employment or other documents.

Discretionary bonuses: The employer may, at its discretion, allocate bonus pay for high performance, a monthly program for the employee, or for good referral of a new employee. Discretionary incentives are not mandatory, and the size of the bonus is at the employer's discretion.

Most businesses, for example, offer year-end or holiday incentives. Whether they are not included in a contract or agreed otherwise, they are conditional incentives.

Non-discretionary bonuses: The employee understands and expects no discretionary rewards. They can be based on a predetermined formula or on factors like attendance. These are usually included in the standard pay rate, stated in the employee's offer letter or employment contract.

For example, for workers who meet certain performance thresholds, an employer offers a compensation pay package. Because the employee knows what it takes to get the incentive that will be a non-discretionary benefit.

The Fair Labor Standards Act (FLSA) specifies that all wages for workers are included in the base salary scale, which is used for calculating overtime pay, although such incentives can be excluded if certain conditions are met:

- The employer will determine if the bonus will be paid.
- The employer can select the incentive number.
- The bonus is not paid or intended to be paid in compliance with any agreement.
- Some workers are excluded from their overtime requirements if they are
- Pay a fixed wage that doesn't adjust depending on time or commitment
- Compensation of at least $684 a week.
- Perform mainly executive, administrative, or technical duties.

Unlike the FLSA wage criteria, excluded workers can be charged up to 10 percent of their salaries on non-discretionary compensation and benefits.

Negotiated Fee Bonus

There are some situations in which a corporation may issue incentive payments. Managers, particularly senior managers, may have contracts requiring the organization to pay bonuses. Such incentives are also dependent on the company meeting clear revenue goals. They may also be dependent on specific factors, such as revenue, retention of workers, or fulfillment of growth objectives.

Executive bonus awards are not necessarily related to results. Contracted bonus pay outside the executive suite is not normal.

Success Bonuses

Many businesses often give incentives to employees below the management level. Such incentives can be dependent on multiple factors.

- **Individual performance:** Workers are measured on the basis of whether their management has accomplished or surpassed its objectives. This kind of bonus can also recognize soft skills, such as leadership, efficient communication, problem-solving, and teamwork that have an impact on the success of the organization.

- **Company objectives:** An employee will receive a bonus based on how well the entire company performed. If an employee had an outstanding year, but the business was not overall good, the employee would not get the bonus. And, if the organization meets its targets, the incentive will be higher.

- **Pay grade:** Generally, you are eligible for a higher bonus if you are paid more money. For example, if an employee is paid $50,000 a year and could qualify for a 5% bonus, they can pay another employee $100,000 annually with a possible bonus of 10%. Pay rating bonuses recognize that a senior employee may have a more significant impact on the performance of the company.

Commissions of Sales as a Bonus

If you are a sales representative (inside or outside), commissions typically represent a good portion of your salary. These are often called incentives but vary from other bonuses because they are directly connected to the sales numbers and usually nothing else.

Instead of individual revenue goals, some companies set team sales objectives. As a team leader, you can receive, if applicable, a portion of the earned commissions and bonus, just like the other team members.

How to Create A More Enjoyable Work Environment

Do the staff and management enjoy their working environment? Do you see a team effort? Are people happy to participate in the organization? Do people show up on time? Are your sick days or holidays outside the average industry? What do the employee turnover rates look like?

Ask the leaders at the organization these questions, it will help determine if members of your team are actually happy to be part of your business. When your team doesn't enjoy their work environment, they become motivated to quit and be unproductive. It's essential that you have a satisfied workforce who feels comfortable, appreciated and valued.

The more pleasant and comfortable your work environment is, the more your people will enjoy their time working for you. Not every business needs to create a "laid back or fun atmosphere", but studies show that it sure does help. The ultimate goal is to help each employee feel work is a safe place for them to build positive, harmonious relationships and complete their work.

Even having the right type of furniture and lighting is an essential aspect of having a pleasant workspace. Everything's needs to be about comfort. Ergonomic chairs are particularly helpful for those sitting at their desks that carry tablets or type pages of documents. It is also beneficial to have a big desk, but if that is not possible due to the limited space, and then file storage cabinets can do so. Having the latest models of business equipment and computers are also a key requirement for a positive experience.

A combination of natural light and indirect lighting systems will be perfect to offset the harsh fluorescent lights. Poor lighting can lead to higher stress levels and has a negative impact on people's health. Good ventilation will help the team members concentrate on their job, especially when they can work under an optimal temperature.

One huge consideration is the break room environment. This is the place most people go to relax, recover and unwind for lunch or after a long day. It's helpful to add a splash of beautiful decor or set a specific mood for this area of the workplace.

Giving Them a Sense of Achievement

Imagine if you knew that in all you tried, you would succeed, wouldn't that make a massive difference for your life? Here are five tips I recommend to improve to shorten your team's path to success:

- Decide exactly what they need do and explain the action steps they need to take within a reasonable period
- Take and continue to measure their actions. Your main goal is to push them forward and proceed
- Determine the motivational factors required to achieving those goals
- Decide on how you the team will be rewarded if they accomplish the goals
- Communicate the meaning behind working on something difficult, but worthwhile

Once you take these key things into consideration, decide on if you need help from upper level management or if this is something you can complete on your own. Plan to resolve and move all psychological barriers that could potentially hinder your advancement in executing this plan. Be sure to keep a log of your team's goals, plans, progress and challenges.

Making continuous improvements as you go along will lead to growth in all your endeavors and you will experience success.

CHAPTER 6

How to Effectively Reduce Sales Team Turnover

How To Identify Areas of Difficulty

If you run a sales team, you will face challenges. This is just a reality. Problems may have natural circumstances (a project has an arbitrary deadline; team members called out of work, etc.) or internal causes (conflicts with individuals). At some point, every team will have at least a few of these problems.

As a sales leader, the goal is to proactively approach these challenges and not wait for things to unfold before administering a response. Here's are six of the most common challenges you may face:

Absence of Identity

When a team member feels like they don't know their role, or what part they play in the bigger picture, they begin to feel unaccountable towards achieving goals. There may display a lack of engagement and effort, tension between team goals and personal goals, or reduce their level of cooperation.

It is essential to quickly develop the organization's decision-making framework. This should include involvement from all of the main stakeholders as well. The leader needs to take a proactive approach to helping each team member understand who they are and what they want to achieve.

Poor Communication

From time to time, members of the team may disrupt or complain about each other. Some sales representatives can be quiet during meetings, hint at issues but fail to follow up to get the correct answers or resolution.

Research has shown that successful teams interact and communicate frequently. If team members don't talk to each other or even talk to you, you may need to get another leader involved to help draw quieter workers out of their shells.

Conflict Resolution

Conflicts cannot be resolved when tensions escalate, and team members underperform when they feel personally attacked or offended. Around half of the tension at work is actually due to variations in team member's personalities.

In some cases, it's essential to get the two parties together and allow them to get a better understanding of each other's viewpoints in order to settle the dispute. One person may be irritated with what they consider their counterpart's inability to do stuff, but perhaps that person is just a creatively fluid individual who struggles with meeting deadlines.

Failure to Participate

When team members are not able to complete tasks, meetings become poorly attended or there's low energy during meetings, something is wrong. Your team may feel like they aren't being listened to carefully, or that the business only cares about profits and not them. Successfully increasing participation is not easy but can be done with strategic planning and inviting the team to contribute their suggestions.

Failure to Build

The team cannot produce new ideas and perspectives and will turn unforeseen events into opportunities if not taught to do so.

Everyone can be more productive with practice, but not everybody is just as innovative. Be sure you appoint a sales leader who will be a visionary and can share ideas that help light up the path in the direction the organization is looking to go.

Poor Leadership

Great leaders are willing to take control and win the confidence of others. A high-performance team should have a leader who is willing to go over and beyond to ensure the team's success. Poor leadership will directly affect the team's morale and reflect on the sales figures.

Ways To Communicate Your Sales Goals

Today, many businesses struggle to consider the challenges and issues that keep their customers awake at night. In order to create an effective sales and marketing strategy, you must master the art of delivering customer satisfaction. In order to thrive in business, it's important to communicate that you can give the customers what they really want.

Most businesses produce goods and services under the premise that the customer is ready for purchase. But that is not always the case. Generating the right kind of leads is crucial to communicating and meeting your sales goals. The marketing team should be executing campaigns that allow the sales team to fill these three buckets:

- **Just browsing for Info** - Not ready to buy
- **Searching for a solution** - Could Buy in the Future

- **Has an immediate need** - Ready to Buy Now
- To begin, filling the buckets, your marketing team should start on the following priorities:
- Figure out what the target audience needs and what it wants.
- Match your solution with the desired outcome
- Sell the solution to them, not the means to do it.
- Find out how to further support their concerns

As marketing qualified sales leads start to come in, make sure you communicate your expectations to the sales team about closing those leads. A sales leader should be in charge of setting specific and realistic deadlines. At this stage, sales goals should be communicated daily, weekly and monthly. Depending on how quickly these leads progress through the buyers' journey, your team should now be able to successfully close more deals.

Here's a list of the most popular methods to communicate your sales goals: email, web conference, video broadcast, in-house or online meeting, internal social media platforms, or through first-line managers.

How To Inspire Confidence, Energy And Enthusiasm

The importance of self confidence in sales cannot be understated. A confident sales person will immediately put any customer at ease. Some people are born with this skill and there are those who still need to work on it. Sales team members who lack self-confidence may show signs of boredom, anxiety, feeling stuck, or dissatisfied with their work.

A great sales leader can help inspire them to continuously improve and bring back their enthusiasm for their work. Here are five tips you can use to start:

- Focus on their areas of strength
- Replace negative with positive reinforcement
- Show examples of how others achieve
- Embrace a growth mindset
- Increase their sense of ownership

Having a high-level of self-confidence, will not only help improve sales performance, but will strengthen your team's social skills and ability to create long lasting relationships in the future.

Now, there will be plenty of times where the well runs dry and your people will feel like they just don't enjoy selling anymore.

That's okay, it happens to the best of us. Here are a few things you can do to inspire enthusiasm and rejuvenate their desire to sell:

- Show them how big of a difference they are making
- Help them to define their purpose on the job
- Share the end goal and rewards to be made
- Show how far the company has come
- Have personal pep talks with them
- Be optimistic and paint a picture of the future
- Integrate their passions and motivations into the job
- Spark their curiosity and belief in their work
- Showcase their unique talents

It's really simple to align your life with what's important when you live and work by a simple set of principles. When a company has defined their core values, it's the sales leader's job to carry them out and shape the sales culture. These core values often have a great impact on your business strategy and long-term profitability. Values like integrity, honesty, trust, accountability, and passion are amongst the most popular adopted by companies of today.

Roles And Responsibilities From The Start

The four fundamental leadership duties of guiding, coaching, helping, and delegating define the particular responsibilities of a leader. Each of these four groups would have a different role. In leadership practice, you need to master skills in all areas to successfully lead others.

Good leadership doesn't just happen; it follows basic laws that cover these four core areas of responsibility. Leadership skills must be learned and established, even if an individual has no natural leadership inclination. When they are mastered and implemented, they make a leader more successful and efficient as he or she learns to work, to direct and guide others towards a collective achievement of objectives and goals.

Building strengths in each of the four leadership positions allows a leader to accurately read all circumstances and know the best way to communicate. The leadership is who will solve or put an end to problems. They are in charge of determining the feasibility of an approach to a mission, the continuity of momentum, and whether it is achieved by the deadline. If you are a leader or manage leaders, there are several ways they can improve their instruction techniques.

Thoroughly explain issues and give the 'why.'

Leaders know early that the best way to obtain their worker's trust and confidence is to describe everything in its entirety. When people understand why something is important or necessary, they are usually attentive to what needs to be done and will agree to take action.

Be present

Leaders are also mindful of the strength of their presence. The sales workforce will feel more motivated to work when the leadership is actually involved in the improvement or guidance process. Leaders should always send the right signals by showing up, making people feel good about their work, and effectively communicating.

Consider all viewpoints

Leaders come from different points of view and usually have dealt with different sets of circumstances, challenges, and solutions. Increasing your workforce's participation and potential for success means carefully thinking about the impact a problem or even a decision could have on all parties.

Continuously Educate

Coaching means that a leader knows where he or she wants to go and stays in charge of the job, but needs to guide others to build a network for mutual help. Coaching instills the drive to succeed and creates a relationship between the coach and those who are under their responsibility. Continuous education motivates workers and changes their attitude about the job. A leader must make an effort to do this every chance they get.

Use the phrase "We"" not "I" in talks

The term "I" is omitted by successful leaders because it represents a personal initiative instead of a shared one. The very meaning of the word coaching implies a team effort. So always think "we" and not "me" when communicating with the sales team.

React to complaints and misunderstandings

Great leaders are able to cultivate the ability to overcome challenges through constructive communication and by producing straightforward answers. Effective coaching relies on complete comprehension of the problem at hand. Leaders should always be ready to provide a 'why, what and how' response to resolve any complaints. Take a moment to process the complaint, decide on the course of action and always thank the individual or customer for their feedback.

Delegate

Leaders know their people and respect them. They know what motivates and frustrates them and their vulnerabilities. Good delegating depends on the ability to choose the right person for a specific task or position. When delegating, it is important to clarify precisely what the leader expects of the empowered individual. They should be able to trust in the person they choose and pick individuals whose skills, experience and perseverance aligns with the task at hand.

Personal Encouragement Strategies

Leaders quite often underestimate the level of encouragement that is required by their team. Much of determining how much and how often to encourage is based on these factors:

- How much does their effort matter, and how good are they going to be?
- How much importance do they attach to the task of achieving their sales goals?

- How do they feel about being thanked for contributions to their team?

- What defines success or failure to them?

- What is their psychological status, i.e., how critical is their performance or achievement for friends, family, or other adults?

- What other matters consume their minds or hearts at the moment?

Matter of context and interpretation

The more your sales team has a history of failed attempts, the more motivation they'll need to make to try and yield successful results. This is because their poor experience of learning has to be resolved. Their history has strong expectations of uncertain success and needless effort, i.e., the essence of discouragement. This phenomenon also arises due to disaffection and alienation at work.

The more extended your sales team is in a failed situation, the higher their negative expectations, and the more support they require. That is the reason it is essential to start developing a culture of achievement at an early stage of their careers with the company.

This trust reservoir helps develop resilience in the face of setbacks and failures. Similarly, we sometimes overestimate the strength of a few achievements in the present; as many shortcomings in the past can weigh them down.

Four Approaches to Personal Encouragement

Encouragement is more than optimistically, saying, "Yes, you can!" What many sales people need is strategic support that all their leaders organize and do so consistently and over time. Here are the steps:

Step 1: Set a reason why the sales person has a mission.

Step 2: Demonstrate how this assignment applies to or is similar to other tasks in which the person has achieved.

Step 3: Demonstrate how the person's specific skills and abilities contribute to the task.

Step 4: Schedule support check-ins with respected leadership to evaluate attempts made to improve and maintain performance.

Performance Improvement Plans

The correlation between strategic priorities and objectives to the development phase is one of the elements most often ignored in any performance management plan. Management typically encourages teams to choose their preference instead of taking the time to identify and pick key development objectives. It leads to a reliance on the media instead of the end results, and the numbers on the charts instead of concentrating on what the company is best for.

The most effective attempts to increase performance occur when management takes the time to address business needs by creating a strategic framework for change. Management must set targets for progress that are explicitly related to the company's strategic objectives. Every goal should be measured with a SWOT analysis and achieved with enhancements to the team.

The first stage is to assess the current state of the organization through a study. The positive and negative factors that drive the company are essential to identify at this level, the key performance indicators, which include financial measures and measures of quality, but also include a number of intangible elements such as employee morale, management capabilities, and organizational structure.

Once the current state of affairs is known, the management team will define the goals for furthering and maintaining the company. Objectives are assessed by applying expectations or parameters to the main performance measures. Another factor is to ensure that the targets are set; time is limited and you have a dedicated person who is responsible for achieving them.

Once the targets are decided upon and accepted, the next step is to define the methods needed to achieve the goal. Such approaches are described initially at a high level, and the output teams can further define them with a range of methods, including problem identification and by conducting a root cause analysis.

For the best results, each output team will arrange a two-day workshop to improve operations, which will tackle a specific problem or opportunity and direct them through the process of identifying and planning activities. A separate workshop should be held for each of the objectives listed. The composition of any output team should be varied and dependent on the level of expertise required to examine the problems relevant to each target.

A straightforward action plan should be the outcome of each workshop. Considerations for developing an action plan include:

- What are the specific aspects?
- How are we to proceed in particular?
- How do we define what, how, and when resources are needed for each move

- What is our end goal and strategy to achieve?
- What are the steps to take?

Once the action plan is drawn up and approved, it's time to take action. Too frequently, the team starts to take action before the proposal has been approved; usually, these results in efforts that boost performance becoming less successful and quickly leads to yet another "flavor of the month" for both staff and management. Taking action requires:

- Discipline in design and development
- Preparedness to avoid or use contingencies
- Proper implementation of the plan's first steps
- Versatility to change activities along the way

The last step is to measure the effect of each action. You have no way to determine the progress you are making without measurements. It's like a road trip with a way to determine your miles. You don't know how far you've come, and worse still, how far you have yet to go.

Effect assessment key points include:

- How are we?

- What are the leading monitoring indicators? (Situation, company operation, people)
- How do we refresh our understanding of the situation?
- What are the results?
- What are the consequences?

This is a cyclical process, and a lot of refinement is required to optimize every aspect of the process. Each phase is correlated with other steps. For the success of the management chain, excellent communication is essential.

Improving Overall Motivation

It is not hard to set simple objectives to enhance self-development and motivation, given that you take three main steps, which will take you to a new stage. These actions are not difficult to follow and will allow you to do things you would have never thought possible. Many times, we are overwhelmed by so many different forms of tips and advice that we forget about some of the most basic things we have the power to do. Here are the top three things leaders do to improve overall motivation:

Inspire your team

Inspiration is the first significant step towards self-improvement and motivation. Your team will be well on their way to substantial self-improvement if they can be inspired. When you find it hard to be driven by something, you first want to concentrate on ways to be motivated. Without motivation, you would have trouble motivating yourself. When you look at life as responsibilities rather than incentives, you are automatically less motivated.

When things your team does every day are seen as responsibilities, you should consider examining their daily habits and find ways to adjust them to their interests. Help them make changes if they are unhappy with their work, work relationships or environment. You will discover that creativity and innovation is inspiring and just adding a little touch can do wonders for motivating your sales team.

Set goals for your team

Goals, sadly, are easier to set than to accomplish. One of the factors that discourages most sales people is the unrealistic standard of setting targets. Setting realistic targets can be the most satisfying measure on the path to experiencing significant improvement in your team's motivation.

Your team will take things more seriously if you have been transparent with your targets. Separate the goals you consider to be more straightforward from those you find to be more challenging. Painting a big picture for them will provide a clear understanding of what you are looking for.

Connect with your team

Some of the most incredible ways to build a clear sense of purpose is to share your experiences with team members who want to accomplish similar goals. Not everybody has the same perspective, and access to a range of other people's thoughts and views will help them master their own skills.

Connecting with others will get you amazing results. You would be gratified at the end of the day because you have the opportunity to share your knowledge and professional insights with the others. Being connected inspires a whole new degree of determination within us, helping us to meet the next day with absolute power and energy. Breaking down barriers to information, having regular staff meetings and growing to be a trustworthy, passionate leader are strategies that won't let you down.

CHAPTER 7

How to Choose:

Mentoring vs Coaching vs Training

Differences Between Them All

Sometimes it is difficult for companies to identify the distinctions between the three concepts. This is because each one is very close and, in many respects, overlaps. There are also substantial variations between the three that can cause them to easily resemble one another.

One of the main differences between coaching, training and mentoring is how they are offered. Typically speaking, most coaches, trainers, and advisors help their clients share their knowledge, experience, and understanding. Everybody is motivated by the same goals and purpose when it comes to teaching, coaching, and mentoring in order to help others achieve their full potential.

Training: A trainer's job is to share his expertise and experience with his trainees. They can do so by a number of methods like reading, writing, drawing, and hands-on content. They are usually a specialist in their profession and offer individual or group instruction. In terms of preparation, you would generally expect to do a final assessment and see how far the client has come as a result of the training process.

Mentoring: This strategy allows the mentor to build a more intimate relationship with the person being advised. In addition, a mentor provides advice and guidance in a wide range of fields. The person will not limit themselves to offering feedback strictly through constructive criticism, but also through frequent communication to advise on reaching goals, direction, and solving problems.

Coaching: Coaching is different from the other two methods, largely because a coach is not always considered an expert. Their job is largely to guide the person being advised to self-discovery. They should be available to help the person find a solution that works for them. They are usually tasked with the responsibility of showing consistent improvement over a specific period of time.

These three strategies have many parallels. Pairing the right strategy with the right people will undoubtedly contribute greatly to your sales team's performance.

Basic Skills and Knowledge Acquisition

Every sales organization who hires new employees should prepare a plan to enhance their basic skills and knowledge of the job. In order to best benefit the organization a leader should weigh out the skills deficit vs potential. Take time to identify which skills need to be developed and fill the gaps as soon as possible. When trying to determine if your team members need training and in what to conduct it, ask yourself the following questions:

- What skills are required for the job?
- Does everyone on the sales team need these skills?
- Can the skills be effectively taught by other employees or will you need a means to train and coach?
- Which sets of skills are needed the most?
- What key skills need to be taught?
- What should the outcome be of these new skills?

Once you've made a final assessment on the skills and knowledge that your people need, proceed to designing a training process that will benefit both the trainee and the company.

The Knowledge Transfer Process

Knowing the role and responsibilities in the training process will help you achieve all of your desired goals.

1. Initial Stages

A trainer has:

- Professional skills that they can bring to help
- The ability to test their skills and experience critically
- The trainee will have:
- Professional goals they need your help to achieve
- A goal-related requirement for the job

2. Communicating Anticipations

A trainer should:

- Create a plan for achieving milestones
- Set realistic training schedules
- Communicate the company's expectations
- Adjust their input to learning and communication styles for each trainee

The trainee should:

- Communicate consistently with the trainer
- Talk to the trainer about their ambitions and discuss how they are meeting milestones and goals
- Adhere to the training schedule
- Tell their trainer their expectations for learning and communication

3. Functioning Together

A trainer should:

- Providing positive feedback and reinforcement
- Draw on and understand the strengths of the trainee
- Be bright and comfortable training
- Assess progress each step of the way
- Be the cheerleader for your trainee as they work towards or accomplish their goals
- Monitoring and track results

The trainee should:

- Listen and engage in the discussion

- Understand that your trainer may not have all the answers
- Assess progress each step of the way
- Accept transformational suggestions
- Be comfortable communicating any shortcomings
- Be willing to celebrate their success
- Update their trainer on their performance

Improve Your Team's Competencies and Capabilities

One of the key functions of your management structure should always include ways to boost competencies and capabilities. A big part of this is being able to measure what's happening and what's not. Key things to measure would be your team's ability to make cold calls, set appointments, assess the quality of a lead and close the deal.

Competency based training is commonly used and can address anything from general sales concerns to individual issues. Sessions may concentrate on a specific skill, for example, communication, teamwork, presentations, and closing sales or anything that you or your team need to improve on. Regardless of how many sessions it takes, the investment can be compensated substantially on a long-term basis. These types of training need to be continuous, not one-time events or else the program will fail.

Communication and willingness to learn is a huge competency that is required by the job. If you combine a group of individuals, you will face obstacles, everything from peer to peer interactions to individual success over team results. You would probably see a related decline in morale and efficiency if you find that your team is not getting along. Continuous coaching can help open back up the lines of communication and build a stronger relationship for all of the team members.

You will see, every member of your team will start to work together more efficiently and create partnerships that help everyone at the organization. Using competency-based training will help the team concentrate on winning deals instead of group disagreements.

Technology has also played a major role in a sales team's ability to do their job. Many teams won't feel they are capable of closing deals if they don't have a way to track their progress effectively. Today, sales focused organizations empower their people to sell more by giving them access to intelligent CRM tools. This will increase their effectiveness when selling and result in higher close rates and a better customer experience.

CHAPTER 8

Sales and Marketing Alignment

How to Map Out Your Customer Journey

Whatever the business is, each consumer has a process before making a buying decision. Understanding the client's paint points will allow you to decide the details you want to deliver and when. The more you understand the customer, the more knowledge and content you can provide to them to improve the likeness of a sale.

Once you understand who the customer is, you can build a sales funnel. The funnel should be designed based on the potential pressure points at each level of the customer journey. Once you build a funnel, you will most likely start to find new pressure points that you would not have known of at first.

Understanding the Target's Priorities

The objectives of your audience are super important to helping you create the right content to target a potential customer at the right time. A potential customer is usually aware that they have a problem but is actively looking for a recommendation or solution to their problem. In order to effectively generate sales leads, your team needs to establish what it is the customer really needs. Is it functionality, convenience, control, accessibility, reliability, or performance they are looking for?

Honestly, it could be all the above. Its marketing's job is to resolve these needs by marketing the solutions that meet their current priorities. The more you understand their priorities, the better you'll be able to sell to them.

What is the Role of Marketing vs Sales?

For many organizations, deciding the roles marketing vs sales will play is a bit confusing. Generally, the role of marketing is to convince and sales is to convert. Marketing's job is to do everything possible to fill the sale pipeline with prospects and potential people who are interested in buying services. It's the sales team's job to do everything possible to close a deal.

Reduce Unproductive Prospecting

The goal of marketing is to not only grab the attention of the potential prospect, but to stimulate interest in learning more and create leads from that entire process. The sales team doesn't want to waste time contacting and following up on leads that aren't truly interested in buying at this time. The marketing team can reduce unproductive prospecting and shorten the sales cycle by simply pre-qualifying leads and assigning them to stages before they get to sales. This can be easily done by adding 'qualifying' questions to the lead forms they use. Asking the right questions will help eliminate people who are not ready to buy and help your sales team work more efficiently.

Enhance Your Sales Processes and Procedures

You will increase efficiency with well-defined processes and procedures by reducing ineffective sales and marketing programs. Don't be afraid to cut programs that aren't delivering expectations or serving your organization. Remember, you are in business to do business. If your current sales or marketing process aren't growing the business, they need to be cut.

Brand Messaging for Everyone

When your brand messaging is being developed about your company's mission, vision and products or services, it's extremely important that the sales team also has access to all key talking points and messages. This is going to help them communicate the company's value proposition and accurately reflect the image and quality of the brands' products and services. Being able to fit the solutions to the customer's expectations is of extreme importance when it comes to accelerating the sales process and closing deals.

CHAPTER 9

Measuring Results and Sales Impact

Planned Activities, Meetings Schedule, Logged Calls

As leaders, it's easy to let time slip away from us. Many of us are wearing multiple hats and are responsible for a lot of moving parts. Sales leaders need to be specially equipped to organize the sales activities of their organization. It's important to centralize all of your activities into a CRM system.

A powerful CRM can help your team seamlessly get through the day and make them much more dynamic. You'll have a full view of all of their meetings, calls, e-mails, assignments, and activity-type reminders to help you quickly locate and prioritize the right activities. All activities generated are directly presented in a dashboard featuring your activity stream. This benefits your entire team to see what their colleagues are up to or what they plan to do in the future. A CRM will also allow your team to see which action items are due today, overdue or due soon.

Performance management is improved when you are able to monitor your success against the tasks you have set. The objective is to gather as much information as you can about your team's qualified leads, scheduled calls, follow-up attempts, time spent cold calling and meetings actually set. Take this information and compare it to the sales results. Decide on which set of activities yield the best results and plan to increase in those areas.

Pipeline Development

A sales pipeline is an orchestrated and visual approach to monitoring several potential buyers through different phases of the buying process. The pipelines are often seen as a funnel, split into the stages of the selling phase of a product. Potential customers are accelerated from one step to another as they progress through the selling process: for example, when contact is made by a sales rep or if they've requested more information, they will get placed in the next stage.

It is a way to see where prospects are going from the lead stage to when they turn into an actual customer. Having a sales funnel is an essential resource for teams who frequently juggle multiple sales opportunities and offers.

Sales managers find value in knowing how well their selling cycle works. As a pipeline monitors the activities of their salespeople and it provides more visibility to the company's sales activities.

Set up the phases based on the activities the sales team does to generate revenue and do whatever it takes to move deals from stage to stage. Take a balanced approach to pipeline construction, and don't be afraid to check if the pipeline seems to require more or fewer phases. Honing the pipeline will help you reach the numbers more accurately. With a simple, workable pipeline, you can find out what drives sales and start making more of them.

Sales Revenue

Sales revenue is the income from the selling of products or services earned by a company. In accounting, the terms "sales" and "income" can and is often used to mean the same thing on an interchangeable basis. It is necessary to remember that income does not automatically imply earned cash. A portion of sales income may be paid up front, and a portion may even be paid by means of credit, such as the accounts due.

Sales revenue can be classified as gross revenue or net revenue on a business's income statement. Net revenue includes all return deductions, unlivable merchandise possibility, and expenses for unrecoverable receipts (also known as "mal debt expenses" that flow into the balance sheet as the doubtful account allowance). On the other hand, gross revenue does not include these deductions.

When measuring results and the true impact of your sales activities, you need to assess how much revenue has been generated. This is usually done by generating reports on how much revenue came in by product line, service line, or by channel. It's also extremely important to review the number of deals lost vs won, the time it took to close and the average deal size.

Every sales focused organization needs to outline their key performance indicators and review them consistently with their team. These are the most important KPI's and can truly be optimized to achieve a better performance:

- How long the sales cycle is
- Quote to close ratio
- Revenue per client
- Monthly calls per sales rep
- Average customer lifetime value
- Percentage of monthly sales growth
- Percentage of leads actually followed up with
- The percent of people achieving their quota

Key performance indicators should always be communicated across the organization, so the salespeople know they are responsible for owning this initiative. Understanding where your team stands with these metrics will easily guide your future business decisions.

CHAPTER 10

Getting the Best Outcome

Signs of Improvement

Each business, whether large or small, strives hard to achieve better outcomes year over year. Companies want to retain their existing clients and generate more in the future. There are few things you need to keep in mind when trying to increase the likeliness that you'll get the best outcome.

- Work efficiently and effectively
- Provide work to your team that is meaningful
- Mindset and motivation is everything
- Refine your techniques
- Set limits and boundaries on your time
- Don't bite off more than you can chew
- 80% action, 20% thinking
- Build momentum based on results
- It's what and who you know

People who engage in sales have a lot to do and it can be a tough job. Since sales activities ten to happen in a fast-paced environment, it's important to pay special attention to the signs of improvements.

Most sales staff spend a lot of time planning their pitch, and their ability to supply product or service knowledge in advance. Sometimes management can make the mistake by thinking more work makes more progress. That's not always the case. How do you know if things are *really* going in the right direction? Progress is usually measured by reviewing the sales performance data. Here are a few questions to ask yourself while evaluating the numbers:

- Have any of the numbers increased?
- Has your position moved forward or backward?
- Do you recognize a higher level of response?
- Has there been a spike in any particular category or segment?
- How much closer are you to meeting your goals or target?

Success is usually measured based on movement. The closer you get to completing a task on target, the better chance you'll have at reaping results. When you find the best way to monitor your progress and the forms of progress you need to pursue, pick how often you will track it. In a sales focused organization, there will be plenty of activities to track progress from week to week.

CONCLUSION

Remember, successful leaders will always break barriers to continue to inspire and create opportunities for their team. Even if you don't fully understand the process, what counts the most is that you are confident in your abilities, you value your relationships and are passionately committed to your work. Leaders aren't built overnight, but compassion, empathy and understanding will help you lead your team to a much better place. Cheers to your success,

-Adella Pasos

www.ingramcontent.com/pod-product-compliance
Lightning Source LLC
Chambersburg PA
CBHW032123250526
R18348000001B/R183480PG45466CBX00042B/3